Tes

Light Come Out of the Closet

"Leslie effectively braids a three-strand cord of innocence, levity, and pain. The way that cord freely weaves in and out of young Roger's relationship with his family, his God, and himself kept me turning pages to discover if it would be his lifeline or his noose."

Andria Flores
Author of *Type A Plans B*

Books by Roger Leslie

Memoir *Light Come Out of the Closet* (2023) Paradise

Calendar book *FLY Book of Days* (2023) Paradise

Writing instruction *From Inspiration to Publication* (2020) Paradise

Spiritual inspiration *Divine Destiny* (2019) Paradise

Movie reference *Oscar's Favorite Actors* (2017) McFarland

Spiritual inspiration *My First Last Year* (2015) Paradise

Character education resource *Teach Me SUCCESS* (2014) Bayou

Performing arts reference *Film Stars and Their Awards: Who Won What for Movies, Theater, and Television* (2008) McFarland

YA biography *Eagle on Ice: The Antarctic Adventure of Teenager Paul Siple* (2008) Vantage Press

Novel study guide and test book *Saurcana Teachers' Sourcebook* (2005) Seaworm

Biography *Isak Dinesen: Gothic Storyteller* (2004) Morgan Reynolds

Motivational book *Success Express for Teens* (2004) Bayou

Novel *Drowning in Secret* (2002) Absey & Company

Library text *Center Stage: Library Programs that Inspire Middle School Patrons* (2002) Libraries Unlimited (co-authored with Patricia Potter Wilson)

Library text *Igniting the Spark: Library Programs that Inspire High School Patrons* (2002) Libraries Unlimited (co-authored with Patricia Potter Wilson)

Library text *Premiere Events: Library Programs that Inspire Elementary Patrons* (2001) Libraries Unlimited (co-authored with Patricia Potter Wilson)

History *Galena Park: The Community that Shaped its own History* (1993) published by Galena Park archivist Sue Elkins Edward (co-authored with Sue Elkins Edwards)

Books available online, in bookstores, and at RogerLeslie.com.

Light Come Out
of the Closet

Memoir of a Gay Soul

Roger Leslie, PhD

Paradise Publishing
Spring, TX
2023

ParadisePublishingHouse.com
RogerLeslie.com

Light Come Out of the Closet / Roger Leslie (1961 –)

>1. Memoirs. 2. Gay Culture. 3. Nineteen seventies. 4. Culture Conflict—Religious aspects—Catholic Church. 5. Depression in adolescence. 6. Self-Esteem. 7. Spirituality.

340 p.

>ISBN 978-1-941680-07-0 (hard cover)
>ISBN 978-1-941680-08-7 (perfect bound)
>ISBN 978-1-941680-09-4 (ebook)
>ISBN 978-1-941680-10-0 (audiobook)

SUMMARY: When a joyful boy realizes he is gay, he fights against family and religious prejudices to reclaim the God of love he learned about in hopes of discovering what it means to be a gay soul. Dewey: 306.76

NOTE: All events described in this memoir were shared through the perceptions of the author. Some people depicted are not identified by their real name.

Edit by Andria Flores (andria@andriaflores.com)
Interior and Exterior Design by Jen Aiken (jen@jvodesign.com)
Cover Design by Deena Rae (eBookBuilders) www.ebookbuilderspro.com
Cover Photo by Angela LaMonte (angela@onlyonceimages.com)

The paper used in this publication meets the requirements of the American National Standard for Permanence of Paper for Printed Library Materials Z39.48-1984.

For every book purchased, Roger Leslie has a tree planted.

First edition.
Printed in the United States of America.

Dedication

to the people in my childhood

who loved me exactly as I was

before I knew how

Table of Contents

I'm Going to Hell

Before I was old enough to articulate them as defining truths, I have known three absolutes:

I love God.

I love my family.

I am gay.

The sliver of the world I knew in childhood consistently supported those first two insights. I was raised by parents so committed to our religious upbringing that Dad worked extra to send my sister, brothers, and me to Catholic school. In my close-knit, Polish-American enclave, the family unit was paramount. Loving God and loving my family came with a guarantee: who I loved loved me in return. Though it remained unspoken, I always belonged. Then I awakened to a frightening suspicion. My third truth—that I am gay—could negate my assumption that love was automatically reciprocal. As the truth of my sexual identity clarified for me, so did the possibility that my family might not love me gay. But an intense terror loomed more threateningly in my waking life as a child and my hours of prayer as a young soul: What if being gay meant that God wouldn't love me either? All the affections and desires for love that felt natural to me, as a child of God made by God's hand in the image and likeness of God, seemed at odds with what the world and my religion suggested was honorable and spiritual.

I have always known I am gay. Even before I understood what that meant, I sensed that I was different from everyone else I grew up around, even my own family. Yet in my stable home with my loyal parents, I felt safe, protected, and, yes, loved. But whether a sign of the era or my culture, love as I recognized it in my childhood home was neither verbalized nor demonstrated with physical affection.

When I was very, very young, I know that my dad held my hand when we walked on vacation because once we lost each other's grip on a packed boardwalk. When I reclaimed the hand, it felt rough, and it pushed mine away. I was shocked to look up and discover I had grasped a stranger's hand. On another vacation we walked so long down sidewalks of Toronto that I dragged beside my father, leaning on his arm as we trudged to our hotel. At the time, I didn't recognize his support as love.

In my family, Dad always encouraged us to forge our own path. "Be a leader, not a follower," he admonished all his children. As a result, my siblings and I were vehemently different. It seemed a requirement in our family to develop our character by finding interests that no one else in the family enjoyed.

Judy, the eldest of us four children, became an accomplished ballerina from early childhood through her teens. It took little time for her to outperform all her peers and become the star pupil of once-famous ballerina Leona Lucas.

My older brother Randy loved—and excelled in—every sport available to a suburban boy in the 1960s. In the basement he hung caricatures of his favorite baseball players. On his desk he displayed an entire collection of walnut-sized pro football team helmets. Most proudly, he cherished a ceramic mug embossed with the front page of the September 18, 1968 *Detroit Free Press* with the headline "WE WIN!" in reference to the Tigers' World Series victory.

Before long, that mug was buried among trophies my brother won—for baseball and football and basketball. Most impressive about my brother was the fact that he overcame an early childhood mobility issue to excel in athletics.

I wanted no part of dance or sports. Instead, I loved visual and literary arts. I didn't just watch movies and television and read books. I studied them, then researched the background and process of developing anything creative. I wrote stories or designed scrapbooks of my favorite celebrities. I loved developing all types of puzzles. I created my own word searches and crosswords. Once, I decided I wanted a jigsaw puzzle featuring my favorite movie, *The Poseidon Adventure*. When no company manufactured one, I assembled a thousand-piece puzzle I had at home, turned it over, and drew my own.

Whatever I loved, I immersed myself in so passionately I didn't care how often others made fun of me. But it did lead me to perceive myself as different from other children.

I could be sociable. I enjoyed playing outside with most of the other children who grew up around me on our cul-de-sac. We raced our bikes or bounced our Super Balls so high in the air we would momentarily lose sight of them. I played with girls more than boys.

Despite our dissimilar interests, Judy, Randy, and I often had similar toys. When Ray came along, he never seemed interested. While very young, Judy had a Barbie, Randy had a Ken, and I had an Allen. Not thinking anything of it, one day I saw neighbors Cathy and Jackie Farchione on their front porch playing Barbies, so I brought over Allen and joined them. They were happy to include me, but other children on our court made fun of me. I didn't quite get why.

So rather than join others in their interests, I took Dad's "be a leader" advice to heart and led activities. Once I decided to teach the younger children on the court how to roller skate. When I designed fliers about my upcoming free lessons ("Fun! Fun! Fun!" promised my tagline), Randy chastised me for planning activities where I was better than others. That wasn't my intention. When I learned something new, I liked teaching others so they could join me.

For a period, I wrote and directed some of the neighbor kids in skits based on TV shows like *Bewitched* and *The Addams Family* and *Here's Lucy*. In time I even created my own show. The season Henry Fonda starred in *The Smith Family*, I developed my own, totally original live-action series, *The Jones Family*. For my pilot episode, I went all out, even redesigning our entire garage to replicate a family house. In one corner where we stored the lawnmower, I turned two sleds covered in beach towels into twin beds where the children of the family would reflect on the events of the show and end it with an uplifting moral.

In time I got more ambitious and wrote stage versions of movies. My cousin and I did a few scenes from *Mary Poppins*, but we never gave a full performance of my play. Eventually my lofty goals outgrew my directing talent. After only a few rough and contentious days of rehearsing my production of *The Poseidon Adventure*, my neighbor and main costar, Jeanette Mamo (I was planning to star in Gene Hackman's role—hmm, maybe Randy had a point) marched into the garage where I was building the scaffolding for Belle Rosen's heroic dive and barked, "I have just five words to say to you." Raising one finger at a time, she counted out each emphatic word. "I. Quit. This. Stupid. Play."

Considering the activities I enjoyed, I wonder how anyone could have missed the fact that I was gay. But in the early 1970s, I don't know that many people even thought about anybody being gay. On his occasional TV specials, Liberace paused between interludes to describe how his mother would remain the woman in his life until he found the right girl, for which he was searching. I read nothing more into that. When Mom and I talked about what we'd read in fan magazines, she usually included a lesson about becoming an honorable man. She told me how starlets' husbands who didn't want to attend premieres entrusted Cesar Romero to escort their wives because he was such a trustworthy gentleman around all women. I never considered the more obvious reason that he was no threat to their marriage.

The little exposure I had to gay characters came from the movie reference books I had begun to collect. Richard Burton and Rex Harrison had starred as gay lovers in a film called *Staircase*, which I could never find in the *TV Guide* movie listing. I also read about *The Boys in the Band* and *Sunday Bloody Sunday*, but they were only telecast on the late, late movie.

The first gays I ever saw on television were not fictitious characters, but authentic people. One evening I stayed up very late with my mother watching television. After Johnny Carson's program ended, *The Tomorrow Show* came on. That night, Tom Snyder featured a lesbian wedding. Personally, I didn't feel one way or another about what I was watching. I was too overcome with the vehemence of my mother's disgust as she grumbled, and watched, but never changed the channel. "They're going to Hell" she told me with the same acidity that she spat the identical statement when Helen Reddy accepted her Grammy for "I am Woman" by thanking "God because She makes everything possible."

The seething intensity of my mother's reaction left me feeling both frightened and dead. I was already confused about sexual identity and God ("She?" I had no idea!). But in those moments it was as clear as the white carpet in the church those lesbians walked down how my family felt about what I was struggling to understand about myself. If I was gay, I was going to Hell.

My Life Was No Sitcom

Loving movies and television distinguished my unique facet in the prism of my family. It was the one area where I knew more than everyone—even my parents.

My mother never had a good memory for movies. To dismiss anything she didn't like, she'd scoff, "Personally, Charlotte, I don't give a damn."

Once I realized she was butchering a line from *Gone with the Wind*, I corrected her. "Mom, her name was Scarlett, and the line is 'Frankly, my dear, I don't give a damn.'"

She dismissed me with a shrug. "Either way, I don't give a damn."

Movie and television escapism had its drawbacks. Experiencing most of my young life through media skewed my perspective of reality. At extended family events, I joined the female relatives who sometimes shared insights about the new Women's Movement. They discussed books like *The Feminine Eunuch* and *Fear of Flying*. I understood none of it. I didn't know what a eunuch was, and I had never even been to an airport, let alone flown in a plane. My only exposure to feminism was the episode of *The Partridge Family* when Keith volunteered the group to sing at a Power of Women rally to please his girlfriend.

Any problem we kids had, my father handled much more stoically than TV dads. Once, I decided to run away from home. I don't remember why, but I'm sure I got the idea from some television show. Whenever a child on a program decided to run away from home, it ended with an emotional reconciliation between the child and parent, with the richer understanding coming from the mom or dad who realized what their child really needed and was willing to change enough to give it to him. It didn't work that way when I planned to run away.

I started by writing a note saying I would leave the next morning. I don't think I gave a reason for my exit. But to back into my point, rather than stating it directly, I emphasized in my note that I was taking our family dog, Bonnie, because "at least *she* loves me."

I figured that someone would find the note, shower me with affection, and convince me not to go. That evening my dad found the note. He responded with an action that startled me. As I lay in my bed, pretending to strategize but really just waiting to see who'd come to my rescue, Dad lay on the bed beside me. He didn't hold me, but he lay so close I could feel his Pall Mall breath as he spoke.

"I read your note."

My mind reeled. My life was a sitcom. This is the point where Andy would tell Opie how much he loved and needed him, or Carol Brady would show Bobby that she also packed a suitcase to run away with him and protect him from the cruel world out there.

"Running away is a very selfish act."

What?

"It makes me think you don't appreciate how good you have it."

Rob Petrie never said anything like this to Richie!

"I work long hours to clothe and feed you. Your mother cleans and cooks all day. While we're knocking ourselves out for you kids, you're spending your time writing a note about how bad you have it."

Even so soon after writing it, I didn't recall saying anything like that in my note. I didn't even include that many details. He was reading something between the lines that wasn't there. I was so stunned by his twisted interpretation that I overlooked the sad implication of how he and Mom saw their roles as parents.

"But—"

Although his words were acrid, his delivery was calm as a monk at vespers. "If you think it's so bad here, you're more self-absorbed than I realized."

I didn't know the word *self-absorbed*. I figured it meant the same as selfish, but it sounded even meaner—especially with Dad's ever-so-mannered delivery.

"I feel especially bad for your mom. She stays home all day taking care of you, and you repay her by writing a note that reveals all this time you're just thinking about how unhappy you are here. That's a fine way to thank her for all she does."

"I do appreciate all she does." *I should know. I spend most of my days doing all the chores with her.*

He shrugged the shoulder not buried into my mattress. "That's not what I read in your note."

My note was a single page printed in the fat letters of a nine-year-old. I couldn't imagine what I said that made him see all that in a few dramatic lines about leaving and taking the dog.

Dad lay in silence looking at me and awaiting my reply. I felt the same lava drip in my chest that always oozed in the confessional when the priest told me I had disappointed God.

"I'll do better."

"For your mom's sake, I hope so."

Then he left me alone to go to sleep. After Dad's revelations about how my selfishness had hurt her, I was afraid to find my mother the next morning at her usual spot at the kitchen table, legs curled to one side, her fingers twirling the loose ashes off the tip of her cigarette on the teeth of her turquoise ashtray.

I stood in the kitchen doorway. Mom was at the table, but so was my sister flicking her long hair over her shoulder to keep it from getting snap-crackle-popped in her cereal. Mom set down her Kool to add another item to her to-do list.

"We have enough Green Stamps to get that cuckoo clock from S & H. Who wants to go with me?"

Judy ate a big spoonful of Rice Krispies so she didn't have to answer right away.

"I will," I offered enthusiastically.

"I know you will." Mom said it matter-of-factly— with neither disappointment nor gratitude. "Jude?" she looked at my sister.

"I've got things to do," was all Judy had to say to end their conversation.

Everything felt so much the same, I didn't know if Mom even knew about my plans to run away. She didn't say anything, and Dad never mentioned it again. Winding our way down Warren Avenue toward the S & H Green Stamp store as the radio echoed with Tony Orlando and Dawn knocking three times on the ceiling, I wondered if I should say something to Mom. I could apologize, but if she didn't even know about the note, then I'd have to explain it, and thus reveal to her how selfish and ungrateful a son I was. But if I left this conversation buried, I knew its bones would rattle unresolved with guilt.

"I'm sorry if I disappoint you, Mom."

Mom froze. Tony Orlando knocked twice on the pipe before Mom clicked off the radio. Then she looked at me. It wasn't a driver's glance. She focused her gaze on me so long,

I started watching the road ahead to make sure she didn't run into anything.

Her breathing accelerated. "Disappoint me?" She clicked an impatient fingernail against the steering wheel. She was either mad because she knew what I meant, or eager to learn what prompted my apology.

Finally watching the road again, she asked, "What did you do to disappoint me?"

I paused to consider. I wasn't thinking about an answer but wondering if her question meant she really didn't know anything about the note.

"Nothing," I admitted because I didn't run away. Dad talked me out of it.

I didn't mean for my answer to sound impertinent, but Mom sure took it that way. "You shouldn't lie to your mother." The finger tapping stopped. She gripped the steering wheel so hard the veins on the back of her hands bulged.

Her reply shook me. I struggled to find words to explain that my "Nothing" wasn't intended to be rude. I genuinely was trying to clarify that I only *thought* something wrong but didn't act on it. Even if it was prompted by my dad's talk, that change of heart showed maturity, didn't it?

Before I came up with a response, Mom repeated her standby comment, "Boża will punish you for it."

Boża was the Polish word for God. Usually, that comment punctuated a conversation with time for me to reflect on what I had done wrong—by her and by God. For the first time ever, I re-engaged the conversation with a simple, but sincere question. "Why?"

Although I genuinely wanted to understand, asking that question on the heels of my last one-word comment stabbed my mother with "Et tu, Bruté" betrayal.

Mom bit her bottom lip. She was wearing lipstick. She never left the house without makeup. Instead of wondering what I should say next to halt this conversation, I imagined the serrated indentations of her front teeth forming a jagged line across her lip when she finally released her bite. "Why do you think?"

Stunned by my beloved mom's cruel tone, I couldn't come up with an answer. Did I disappoint her that much merely with my sitcom dramatics of writing a note about running away? Had she seen the note and felt betrayed? Had I irrevocably let her down? If I did *anything* to make my mother think I didn't love her, then I couldn't love myself.

That was ultimate betrayal because I loved no one more than my mother—including me.

"Well?" Her tone softened from the last question. She wanted an answer. Maybe she was searching for a way to understand me. That would be love. I could live with that hope.

"Because I'm self-absent?" I thought that was the mean word my dad used to describe how selfish I was being for thinking about running away. My mother's confused expression suggested I got it wrong.

I was about to clarify my answer by telling Mom about the note when her expression transformed like overheated clay. It shifted from confounded to furious. "Are you being sarcastic with me?"

My throat tightened. I couldn't breathe. I felt as if someone had jammed a tennis ball down my windpipe. How could my mother even think I would be so disrespectful to her? I loved my mom and wanted nothing more than for her to love me. Impulsively, imploringly, I said, "Mom, I'm a good boy." When the words spilled out, I felt something worse than if my mom had slapped me. Tears trickled down my cheeks.

Mom hated such barren emotion. From her boys especially, whom she was raising to become solid men, such vulnerability was inexcusable.

"Roger." My name only had two syllables when I was in trouble.

When Mom was happy with us, she referred to each of her kids with a sweet, effortless syllable. "Jude. Ran. Rog. Ray." When frustrated or fed up, my mother enunciated our names with a hammered emphasis on the first sound. "Jū'dy. Răn'dy. Rɒ'jer. Rāy'mənd."

She dropped the hammer on those tears.

"Only babies cry." She handed me a tissue. "You're not a baby anymore."

I felt like one. Last night with Dad lying beside me in bed, I felt foolish and guilty for writing the note. In the car with Mom, I felt even more foolish and guilty for crying about it. Then I changed. When I wiped away the tears, I sensed the futility of pleasing my mother. I didn't know how to express to her what I was feeling, in part because I couldn't even identify the feelings myself very well. I felt bad in a hopeless, vacuous way. I had not run away but managed somehow to disappoint both my parents. I'd never seen a TV episode, or even a PG-rated movie that ended so unsatisfyingly!

I didn't feel the full impact of my interactions with both parents until I went to bed that night. As my grandmother, whom we called Baka, had taught us, we always prayed before we went to sleep. Spending the night at her house when we were very little, we'd get to lie down, tucked under her pink chenille bedspread, and pray as she sat beside us. She would say a prayer in Polish and we'd add one in English. By the age when I cried for the last time in front of my mother, I had shifted from praying at home kneeling beside my bed to lying face up, snug under the green paisley print of my quilt. Until that night, I always assumed that my words went upward to the Heavens somewhere above me.

When I prayed after that unresolved confrontation with my mom, I stopped believing that God heard me. It wasn't a conscious decision, but it was as clear and finite as a period at the end of a sentence. If I couldn't express myself well enough for my own parents to have any idea what I was really thinking or feeling, what effect could the silent recitation of memorized prayers have on God?

In that moment, I felt alone. In the physical world, I had my family. In the entertainment world, I could get lost in movie or TV characters, or the lives of celebrities I read about in Rona Barrett's *Hollywood* or *Gossip*. In the spirit world, I was taught that God watched over me like the guardian angel hovering over the chubby little children in Mary Jane shoes crossing a bridge in the paintings above Baka's guest bed.

After my almost-running-away incident, I was convinced neither of my parents understood me. I was not selfish as Dad said. I just didn't know how to ask for a demonstration of affection. I was not still a baby, despite tears that betrayed me to my mother. In two separate scenes, where they might even have been responding to the same information about me, they seemed to be on the same side against me. My relationship with my parents defined my life as a boy and shaped my perception of love—from them and even from God. Now, I didn't trust any of them, or myself.

Where is God?

We called my maternal grandmother Baka because one of her first grandchildren couldn't enunciate the b-sh sound in the middle of the Polish word for grandmother, *babcia*. Baka was a whirlwind of ever-accelerating contradictions. She was tall and imposingly strong. In her sixties, she was pushing her manual lawnmower across her backyard because, even in unison, all four of us kids couldn't budge it. The blades jammed. She gripped the neck of the mower and lifted it as if it were light as a whiskbroom. Her bicep taut, she held it in midair with her left hand while unjamming the blades with her right. Yet she was asthmatic, and sometimes didn't have enough breath to walk to the corner store at the end of her street for milk and bread.

Her emotions were equally mercurial. One Easter she was in such a good mood she literally bounced off a wall.

Noticing my cousin Scott slouching, she pushed her heavy kitchen table away from the wall to press her back against it. "This is how you practice good posture," she boomed, her shoulder blades flat against the drywall. She pounded her chest, "a man should walk like he owns a room." Then she pushed herself off the wall with her buttocks to catapult into the middle of her dazzled grandchildren.

Sometimes, when she spent long periods home alone, depression would grip her so unrelentingly that she'd lock herself inside her house with all the lights off. In that state, nothing could move Baka, not even my mother banging on the door and pleading for a response just to make sure she was okay.

Around kids, especially her grandchildren, Baka was all decisive energy. She amazed my parents and aunts and uncles by regularly babysitting four infant grandchildren at once. She used a sheet to tie some of them in their highchairs while she changed or fed the others. Her unique system of tending to all four simultaneously was as innovative and effective as Henry Ford's assembly line.

One-on-one time with Baka was highlighted by comforting scents and insights. Especially on Fridays when Catholics still didn't eat meat, Baka would fry up thin, crispy-edged potato pancakes. She'd turn the lazy Susan on her table for me to reach the sugar and never reprimand me for pouring enough on my pancakes to kill a diabetic. Late at night, she would shake up a mound of popcorn in her iron skillet and drizzle melted butter over it with the verve of Jackson Pollock.

Bedtime always included a tender moment of her sitting with me to say my prayers. In the painting over Baka's shoulder, barely distinguishable in the shadow of her night light, I would watch the hovering angels above of the young boy and girl crossing a footbridge as I prayed. I always assumed those children represented my older brother and sister. I wondered if, in a painting of the same series, I would be following with an angel of my own.

My first spiritually curious moment occurred when I was a preschooler walking alone with Baka along the pockmarked sidewalk between her house and the corner store. Astir with a gentle summer breeze, the Michigan sky rustled the massive trees that made her neighborhood seem large and old and solid, much as I perceived Baka. Through thick layers of leaves, a gargantuan beam of light swept a broad circular motion around the sky then disappeared. A few seconds later, the beam repeated that same rounded journey.

I stopped in awe and waited for it again. When it reappeared, I pointed, "Look, Baka. It's God."

We stood there until the beam came round again. Then, unfazed, Baka shrugged. "That's not God, that just a spotlight." She took my hand and resumed our walk as if what I had observed meant nothing.

Until I watched a Hollywood movie premiere on late night television a few years later, I really didn't even know what kind of spotlight Baka meant. I think the TV special featured Elizabeth Taylor, and the scene with the spotlight seemed as spectacular as the film being premiered, *Around the World in 80 Days*. Looking movie star-defining gorgeous, Taylor sauntered across the red (actually inky gray on our black-and-white television) carpet on the arm of the film's producer, and her husband, Mike Todd. Punctuating both sides of the screen, two huge barrel drum lights shot rotating beams large and bright enough to light the Hollywood hills. I couldn't imagine what kind of premiere might have happened in Detroit the night Baka and I walked her neighborhood, but at the time, that thought didn't occur to me.

Instead, I felt stupid. I don't know where I got the idea that the spotlight was God. I don't think anyone ever told me that. I suspect I deduced that fact from seeing pictures of Jesus with similar small beams silhouetting His head in many of my prayer books. Such images also dominated the shiny color insert pages depicting Old Testament characters in my book, *The Bible Story Library Illustrated, Volume I.* During our walk, I was too embarrassed to question Baka. But her comment that distinguished for me God from a mere spotlight led me to wonder for the first time, "Then where is God?"

Love is Not Reciprocal

Baka hovered in the periphery of a more painful, defining memory that occurred at her side door when I was still a toddler. From birth, I adored my mother. Since my earliest years, I always wanted to be with her. No matter what she needed to do, I wanted to run errands with her. Our first stop one day was to Baka's house. To my shock, after only a few minutes there, my mother casually mentioned that I was to stay with Baka while Mom ran the rest of her errands alone. I stood there stunned as my mother grabbed her purse and dashed to the door leading to Baka's driveway.

I raced after Mom. She closed the door so fast it slammed. Although I was strong enough at that age to turn the doorknob myself, I was too small to reach the deadbolt my mother managed to lock. Through the window I could see her point a disciplinary index finger and hear her demand, with more frustration than compassion, "You stay here with Baka."

I was beside myself with rage. Still calling for my mother as she disappeared down the driveway, I burst into tears. Holding onto the knob, I stomped up and down until my little feet burned and I bawled until my throat hurt.

Only in retrospect did I consider how my reaction must have impacted Baka. I loved Baka. Some of my best memories from childhood included laughing at her jibes. Once, while Mom drove Baka and some of us kids to check on my Aunt Bev, Baka looked at the car ahead of us and quipped, "Are those pillows on the ledge of that guy's backseat? What is he, some kind of a fairy?" Not really understanding the joke, I laughed with everybody else. Only later when I knew myself better did I feel the sting of her comment's personal repercussions.

A few years later Baka and I built a tender bond. On consecutive New Year's Eves, I was the only grandchild with no plans, so I stayed alone at Baka's. She would go to bed about 10:30 but leave her bedroom door ajar so she could hear me. At midnight, I would call from the living room chair around the corner from her bedroom, "Happy New

Year, Baka." She would reply, "Happy New Year, honey," and go back to sleep. To this day, it is the single memory of Baka that always catches in my throat.

Whether my outraged toddler reaction to staying with her hurt Baka's feelings, I never knew. But I'm sure it made clear to her, as it did to anyone because I was so unabashed in my devotion, how much I loved and needed my mother as a boy. Except for that one incident, Mom always took me to run errands with her on Saturdays. It was a ritual I relished, mostly because I had Mom to myself.

All of us kids together tended to seem too much for her. Although my mother certainly had opinions about many people who were going to Hell, Mom never doomed us to that fate, no matter how we frustrated her. When we children got too silly, or seemed to be having too much fun, she had one of two predictable responses. "Laughing comes to crying," she would warn. If our jokes bordered on the irreverent (or as irreverent as Catholic grade school children could get), she would chastise us with, "Boża will punish you for that." She never intimated that God did anything nice, but He'd get you for sure if you displeased Him.

Despite apparent issues with God and religion that she never discussed with us, Mom offered her version of religious insights meant to be helpful beacons of wisdom. I got most of them one-on-one with her. One bright spring morning when she and I rode down Warren Avenue to Mom's seamstress' house, I saw a deformed young man hobbling down the sidewalk.

"Look," I told my mother. I was so young at the time, I didn't realize it was rude to point, even from inside a car.

She used it as a teachable moment. "Do you know what to say when you see someone like that?"

I didn't.

"You say, 'There but for the grace of God go I.'"

"Oh," I said, not realizing she wanted me to repeat it.

"Say it. 'There but for the grace of God go I.'"

I repeated it. We continued our ride in silence. I'm not sure what I was meant to feel. But the phrase made me feel as lowly as I did every mass when we all had to declare, "Lord, I am not worthy to receive You, but only say the word and I shall be healed." The two phrases felt the same to me. Either way, it was only by the whims of an apparently random or capricious God that I wasn't that poor young man physically disabled for life.

Did it matter that I strove to be a good boy? It mattered to my parents. When I behaved in ways they deemed appropriate for a little gentleman, as I was trained to be (especially in public), they were pleased. Nothing made them prouder than when strangers approached us as my family dined at restaurants and praised my parents for raising such well-behaved children.

One-on-one, I strove to sustain my mother's attention and affection. We dropped off clothes to old Mrs. Skinnell, who ran a seamstress service out of her home. I liked her because I felt sorry for her. She hobbled around her sewing machine, swinging one unbendable leg around like a croquet mallet from having had polio as a child. *There but for the grace of God*, I thought, and felt appropriately guilty for being healthy when she was not.

We called Mom's seamstress "Mizz Skinnell" because three "s" sounds in a row buzzed from our lips like confused wasps. She never minded. In fact, she was one of the kindest adults I knew. Instead of dismissing me, like most grown-ups, she always smiled warmly at me, and offered me homemade gingersnaps from a ceramic cookie jar on her counter.

I'd turn to my mother for permission.

"Take one," she'd shake her head affirmatively.

I thanked Mizz Skinnell as my parents had taught me, secretly wishing one day she'd make chocolate chip cookies instead. She never did.

At Tele-Warren Bakery Mom stocked up on fresh loaves of poppy seed bread, Russian rye, dark pumpernickel and, when in season, egg bread with sweet white raisins. Our final stop was at the Kowalski deli farther down Warren Avenue. Mom selected a variety of cold cuts for the family to eat during our lunch break from Saturday chores. She'd buy hard salami, New York ham and boiled ham (my dad's favorite), and olive loaf that looked like illustrations of amoebae in my science textbook. On different Saturdays, Mom alternately bought strange looking choices that only she ate and could pronounce. The squat Polish lady sliced krakowska, labelka, and sadelki. They all smelled like garbage disposal backwash.

When it came to eating, I had little imagination, and taste buds that furrowed my parents' brows. My Saturday lunch selection was usually bologna, with ketchup, on white bread.

Unlike Mizz Skinnell, who always offered me a cookie, my mother did not regularly buy me a special treat on our errands, even though I was the only one of the kids accompanying her. When she did, it made the gesture more special. The counter beside the meat display at Kowalski's overflowed with more candies than our entire neighborhood of kids could gather after an evening of trick-or-treating. Occasionally, out of the blue while waiting for the Polish baba to finish slicing and wrapping the meats, Mom would see me studying the candy selections and, in the same tone she instructed me at Mizz Skinnell's, would say, "Pick one."

Whatever I selected, Mom would tell the candy counter lady she wanted four. One of Mom's greatest traits was her sense of fairness. She never did for one of her children without doing the same for the others.

That sense of fairness was both inspiring and confusing. I never questioned or hid how much I loved my mom. She was my favorite person in the world. Unflinchingly, I didn't care who knew it. When they wanted to hurt my feelings, some neighborhood kids would call me a mama's boy. Instead of embarrassing me, it inflated me with pride. I liked being my mother's boy. Because of all the attention I lavished on my mom, I sensed we had a special bond. Overtly, though, she wouldn't play favorites. Although I assumed she *had* to love how much I loved her, she never said, to me or anyone, that my attention to and affection for her made me more special to her than her other children.

When I was very little, I didn't think of love as relationship. Maybe my mind couldn't conceptualize beyond my ego-centric focus on loving my mother. But as I got older, I noticed a mental shift in me that affected me emotionally as well. I wanted to sense how much my mother loved me. But my efforts to gain her more intimate attention always failed.

As a boy, I was forever testing myself with new, self-imposed challenges. When reading and re-reading my books became commonplace, I started memorizing their content. Christmas of 1970, my Aunt Leona bought me what I wanted most: a book about the U.S. Presidents. I memorized every President from George Washington to Richard Nixon. Then I committed to memory their political parties, and then the years they served. When I got to the point where I could recite every First Lady's name, I knew I'd taken the challenge too far. Mom knew I loved studying the Presidents, but when I tried to impress her with my abundant knowledge, she consistently replied, "I don't trust politicians" until I stopped talking to her about them.

A few summers later, I was over politics and completely committed to movies. Instead of playing outside with the neighborhood kids, I spent hours sitting alone in the living room on my mother's brown tweed swivel rocker memorizing aloud every Oscar-winning movie and performance from my recently-purchased *The New Hollywood and the Academy Awards* paperback. Mom was not thrilled when I started reciting to her the winners, year-by-year, from 1927 to 1971. Of course, in this way, Mom was not unique. I learned pretty quickly the fastest way to clear a room was to start rattling off names of Oscar-winning actors like Emil Jannings and Joseph Schildkraut and Katina Paxinau, most of whom the average moviegoer never heard of.

In truth, I didn't care if most other people were not interested in what mattered to me. But I hungered for my mom's encouragement. Mom could be very supportive and even effusive with her excitement about her children's achievements—if she initiated the praise. Try to draw it from her and my mother responded with an emotional dodge.

When my intellectual acumen didn't impress her, I thought maybe my creativity would. Once, I decided to develop my drawing skills. On tracing paper, I created a scale grid and overlapped a still of *Who's Afraid of Virginia Woolf?* from my movie reference book entitled *A New Pictorial History of the Talkies*. Square-by-square, I meticulously worked to reproduce the image of Elizabeth Taylor and George Segal on the couch as Richard Burton approached from behind. With laudable accuracy for my age, I managed to recreate the objects in the living room—the branching pattern of the sofa, the cluttered bookshelves. But I had no concept of portraiture, so I saved the faces for last. Because George Segal was in profile, I needed only to get the size and contour of his nose correct to create a manageable facsimile of him. For Burton, I had the advantage of his wearing dark-rimmed glasses and stepping into the scene so far in the background that, proportionately, he was very small. Emphasizing his eyewear and suggesting the tight scowl of his lips sufficed in depicting Burton, who in this scene was being humiliated by another of Taylor's cruel stories about his character.

I spent the most time on Taylor. Splayed like windmill fans on the sofa, her limbs were easy to reproduce. But I struggled intensely with Taylor's face. Trying to get her eyes was especially difficult. Finally, I settled on the closest I could get them and proudly shared the completed sketch with my mom.

"You know what movie this is?"

She didn't venture a guess.

"*Who's Afraid of Virginia Woolf?*"

"Oh, yeah," my mother smiled.

I was elated! My mother rationed compliments like World War II sugar coupons.

"I had the most trouble with Elizabeth Taylor," I confessed, basking in her attentive focus on my picture. *Maybe I DO have artistic talent!*

"I can tell that's Elizabeth Taylor," she affirmed.

"Really?" I was thrilled. I thought my image of Taylor was the worst, and yet my mom even recognized her.

"Oh, yeah."

"How?" I wanted specifics. Was it her lips? I thought I did pretty well forming them into the lemon-wedge shape of her mouth. Could it have been her graying coif? I spent much time blending those swirls and shades. Who knows, maybe I had captured the faraway glint in her eye better than I thought.

Mom pointed to the two simple lines that formed Taylor's bent right leg. "It's the way you drew her knee."

I studied my sketch in confusion before looking up to see the glimmer of irony in Mom's smile. She didn't know the movie still and didn't recognize a single figure in it.

At first I tried to rationalize that she wasn't making fun of me.

I couldn't imagine why she would insult my attempt to draw that scene from *Who's Afraid of Virginia Woolf?*, but I was convinced that was her intent.

Eventually, I knew better than to forage for my mother's approval. The more blatantly I strove to get closer to her, the more creative ways she found to avoid indulging what came to feel like futile neediness.

In this instance, I didn't feel uniquely slighted. My mother remained equidistant from all of us children. She loved us, no doubt, and dedicated our entire childhoods to providing for us and caring for us. Yet even when I was very young, my mother seemed weighed down like Atlas by unhappiness that no amount of coddling or attention lifted.

When opportunities came (or she created them) to get a respite from being around us kids, she savored them. Some Friday nights in spring and autumn, Dad would take us to the Dearborn Drive-In for a double feature. Mom seldom joined us. As we left her home alone, I felt sad for her. I couldn't imagine why she wouldn't want to do something as entertaining as watching movies snuggled in a car with Dad and her four fun kids.

During quiet hours in church—sometimes alone after confession and more often when I stopped paying attention to the Sunday homily—I recognized how my relationship with my mother shaped how I perceived and related to God. God loved me, as I was often reminded by the nuns and my relatives. But like Mom, God was consistent but distant. Whenever Mom would scold us with, "Boża will punish you for that," I suspected that, like Mom, God strained under the weight of discontent. Mom didn't allow herself emotional closeness with us kids, perhaps because we disappointed her for being kids who often acted like kids instead of the ideal children we could sometimes be at restaurants for the length of one fancy meal. In that same way I suspected that God kept His distance from us because we were merely humans unworthy to receive Him. Even if He said the word (and what word was that exactly?) so that we could be healed, from that perspective weren't we still the same creatures unworthy of Him?

Further, I wondered why God would create a humanity unworthy of Him? One of the only reference points to help me answer that query were school projects. When embarking on creative assignments (the results of which I stopped sharing with my mom after the Elizabeth Taylor crack), I always had grand visions of the fruits of my labors. My mind would imagine a dazzling art project, or a beautifully executed essay that formed words at just the right pace and cadence to thrill the teacher who would read it. But what I painted, in colors or words, never appeared on paper with the same magic or majesty of the original inspiration. I wondered if God had grand imaginings of what people would be like once He created them, but then saw Adam and thought, *Ew*. Being a good sport, I suppose, God kept trying, and gave it another shot with Eve. Looking at those results might have generated a defeated little "ugh," after which He wiped the clay from His hands and left Adam and Eve to fend for themselves while God went back to the drawing board or simply concluded that more effort was futile.

In the religion of my youth, that scenario seemed plausible, and wholly disenchanting. As I had with my mother, I wanted to feel intimately close to God. I wanted to please Him so much I helped carry the weight of his discontent like Simon of Cyrene carried Jesus' cross the rest of the way to Golgotha. Somehow as my mother couldn't, I wanted God to stop reveling in the breaks from being with me. In my young mind, where God was perfection, He could never reciprocate or even relate to the need I felt for Him. As I understood it in my youth, love was not reciprocal, but needy and insecure. Ultimately, it could only lead to a loneliness that would define my teens, cripple me temporarily, and seem only relievable by death.

That perspective almost killed me. In distant retrospect, I can see now that it wasn't just realizing that I was gay that made me consider killing myself as a teen. Until I reached puberty, I didn't appreciate the vacuous need of escape. At the time, the reckless and unforgiving 1970s, accepting that I was gay also required acknowledging what I thought my world said about how wrong and sick and cursed I was. That painful realization sometimes numbed me into an emotional paralysis, and more often set a fire in my soul to flee—from life, from myself, and mostly from God.

Oedipus Regina

My mother was not happy. It was my joyful challenge throughout childhood to try to make her so. To some degree, I could. I imagine when it didn't saturate her to the point of annoyance, my constant, worshipful presence must have been gratifying. What mother wouldn't want a child who adored her? I didn't care how unpleasant the task. If Mom would let me spend time doing it with her, I was game. The first time she mopped the newly tiled basement floor, Mom said the mop didn't get it as clean as she wanted. With two buckets, two hard-bristle brushes and Mom's own cleansing concoction, which had as many ingredients as her homemade stew, we spent the entire afternoon on our knees scrubbing that floor. Instead of resenting my siblings for having (or, more likely, finding) something else to do that entire time, I basked in the notion that I alone was the loyal child who would spend a day just like this with her.

I admit to feeling disappointed that, even when we finished, she still scoffed at the less-than-perfect results. It was even more defeating when, as we reached the last section of the basement, Dad came home from work, saw us on our hands and knees, and insisted there was a much smarter way to solve this problem. The next day was Saturday. Dad, who was an architect and builder, secured from one of his building sites an industrial strength electric floor cleaner with brushes the size of Billie Jean King's tennis trophies. In less than an hour, he accomplished what Mom and I could not after an entire sweaty day of dunking and swirling and splashing and scrubbing.

Dad had no way of knowing how defeated his easy solution made me feel. In that instance, I discovered that my motivation for clinging to my mother had evolved sometime in my youth from needing to be with her to wanting to win her love by making her happy. Through my still-brief lifetime of observations, that was a feat Dad rarely achieved. Somehow in my developing brain, I determined that I could find happiness by creating it for my mother in a way my father seldom did.

A traditional therapist might call it an oedipal complex. It was oedipal, but so clear and blatant, there was nothing complex about it. Although my mother was not political, she did vote—but only to cancel out my father's choice. Whoever he was for, she voted against. Or so she always claimed. Once she learned that the courts used voter registrations to summon jurors, my mother threw away her voter registration card. To my memory, she never received a notice for jury duty.

My mother's often unspoken, and occasionally seething, contentiousness toward my father inspired me as a child. In my earliest years, I needed my mom. Every effort to be around her I did solely for me. In time, my motivation shifted to pleasing her—especially when I sensed that my father had disappointed or annoyed her. I noticed a pattern. When my dad was around, my mother was not herself. Perhaps in that disingenuousness I recognized a vulnerability of which I instinctively took advantage. When my mother was unhappy with my father, I redoubled my efforts to be what I thought she wanted. I was lured by her unhappiness, and naïve enough to believe that I could heal it.

From that perspective, I subconsciously distanced myself from my dad. In my mind, though I could never see how, he caused her emotional pain. Loyalty to my mother developed in me an animosity toward my dad that he never deserved. To his credit, and my good fortune, he didn't let it change how he treated me. As he had always been with all his children, he was kind and fair with me. Interestingly, when Mom wasn't around, my dad and I had some wonderful times. He often took my younger brother Ray and me to the movies. When my mom left for a weekend with her bunco club or bowling team, Dad would take us to dinner at the Howard Johnson's on Telegraph Road or buy us double-scoop cones at Stroh's Ice Cream Parlor.

Alone, Dad and I talked movies. When I expressed interest in becoming a writer, he brainstormed plot ideas, or provided feedback on excerpts I'd share with him. Once over dinner at that Howard Johnson's, I noticed a frail woman whose old eyelids had formed taut little canopies above her lashes. I asked my dad to look at the lady and help me come up with words to describe a feature I had never seen on anyone else. My dad did that with me, and for me.

When Mom returned, so did my sense of loyalty to her. I directed my attention to her, not my dad. Something disorienting happened when the travel circumstances reversed and my dad was gone for an extended business trip. Once he left, Mom reveled in the attention I gave her. It was summer, so I could be with her every waking hour, always doing what she, not I, wanted. That week, I felt grown up. Because Mom seemed pretty happy the entire week, I also felt quite accomplished. I loved my mom enough to make her happy.

That interpretation of love paralleled my perception of God. As I understood the lessons of my Catholic upbringing, God was like my mother. He was eternally unhappy. In order to earn His good graces, I had to work nonstop doing what I thought (because He never expressed His needs to me any more clearly than my mother did) would make me pleasing to Him. Throughout that period in my life, it never occurred to me that maybe God acted more like my father—kind and fair, no matter how far off my assessment of my relationship with Him really was.

When my dad returned from that long trip, Mom's behavior stole my breath like an unexpected gut punch. As soon as my dad walked in the door, my mother dismissed me to bathe my father in her attention. While, unnoticed, I struggled to catch my breath, my parents basked in their mutual focus.

I was confounded. What had I done? How was Dad now different from the man she grumbled about while he was gone? What happened to the reward for following Mom's rules, indulging both her interests and whims? I felt used.

Perhaps because I was still too young to distinguish my parents' authority from God's, I felt similarly used by God. Except for some academic faltering in middle school, I was a devout rule-follower. In earnest, I strove to be a good boy who culled the deeper insights from my catechism lessons and built my character on them. I obeyed the adults in my family and at school. I took to heart the commandments, even before I had any life experience to apply them.

I went to confession regularly. Afterward, I didn't just rattle off my penance prayers. While reciting each "Hail Mary," I examined my soul to figure out why I was sometimes mean to my little brother, or what sparked such frustration with Grandma Leslie that I would sass her.

Being obedient helped me feel good about myself. But I recognized also that I was obedient because I wanted to be loved. On one level, there was no doubt. My family life was stable. My parents were constants. We had dinner as a family every night, together around our kitchen table. We always had decent clothes that my mother painstakingly cleaned. She took hours ironing every layer of lace in my sister's Easter dresses, and even scrubbed the boys' socks and shoelaces on a faded old washboard to make them gleam.

True to their Polish heritage, my parents were doggedly hard-working. My father stayed late at his office most evenings, so we ate our dinner later than the other families in our neighborhood. Usually, Mom was miffed at Dad for requiring her to keep the meal warm because, once again, he came home later than she expected. Still, once the evening conversation started, there was constancy and stability.

With her trademark rag—a torn fragment of a sheet—draped over her shoulder, my mother was obsessive about cleaning our house. Other people's annual spring cleaning was a monthly ritual for my mom. She made sure we all helped. But we kids felt secure, and had fun, and could break Mom's intensity with a laugh.

Once when my mother watched Randy limply polish the chrome switch plate in the bathroom, she instructed, "Put some elbow grease into it!" Randy was usually serious like my dad. But he made us all laugh when he wrapped the rag around the bend in his arm and continued shining the plate with his elbow.

When preparing a meal for guests one evening, Mom told me to get a serving dish.

"Where is it?" I asked.

"Down there," she pointed, "with the platters."

I opened the cupboard and melodiously belted out, "Uh-uh, o-only you—" I shut the cupboard and stopped singing. I opened it again and resumed, ". . . can make this change in me." I turned to Mom. "Wow. The Platters *are* in this cupboard!" My mother's approving laughter washed over me.

Despite my psychosexual confusion, in such contexts, I knew love. But I didn't have the insight to look for God in such ordinary circumstances. Like tuning into the right radio station, I thought I could only find God at solemn frequencies. Nothing was more solemn than the hours of 12:00 to 3:00 on Good Friday.

Not-So-Good Fridays

Between noon and 3:00 pm every Good Friday our house bore the quiet, sad reverence of a church. "Those are the hours that Jesus suffered and died on the cross for us," my mother would remind us every year. Then she would instruct us to get the prayer books issued to us when we made our first Holy Communion so we could kneel at our living room sofa and pray throughout those hours.

I can picture Judy and Randy leaning over the cushions, rosaries in hand, moving bead-by-bead around the clusters representing the various Mysteries as their lips moved to the "Hail Mary" and "Our Father" and "Apostles' Creed." I loved my plastic-covered prayer book with the snap-shut side pocket that held my rosary. Unlike most books with regular paper pages, this one, with its full-color illustrations of Jesus and Mary and miracles, had thick pages. With their red outlined sheen, they smelled of liniment and sacrifice. (I was always grateful that they didn't smell of cat pee like some of the most expensive movie reference books in my collection. Imagine the poor paper mill workers who had to smell *that* all day.)

I'm not sure what I liked best about this prayer time. It was about the only activity all year that Judy, Randy, Ray, and I did in unison. Because we were all praying independently, there was no disagreeing or bickering, or bossing around the overly sensitive brother with no backbone. I'd look over at my siblings in prayer. Judy's rosary beads were white ovals. In the light, the opalescence revealed colors not visible with only a quick glance. Randy's were a round, dull onyx. Mine were just plastic. Unlike their rosaries, which had a bit of heft, mine was almost weightless. But my beads were cut with facets. When I turned them in the light, they would sparkle. Such observations indicated that perhaps I was not so fully immersed in prayer during these long hours.

But sometimes I was. I know I was always an unconventional child. Case in point: I savored this prayer time—at least some years, and for the length of time I had the focus and patience to remain still and pray. I might begin by reading the Stations of the Cross in my prayer book or reciting familiar prayers such as the "Our Father." Occasionally I tried not to just rattle off the words to the prayers as my father did when leading us through Grace before meals.

Once during dinner we impersonated his tempo and speed. "BlessusoLordandthesethygifts . . . ."

He grinned. "Really? That's what I sound like?" The next day he enunciated each word so slowly, the meatloaf cooled by the time he said, "Amen." Turns out my dad had more of a sense of humor than I knew.

Of course, my father was working during the Good Friday hours we prayed, so he wasn't there at the couch praying with us. Come to think of it, although she was home, neither was Mom. It was too late for her to be savoring her usual breakfast—a glass of Coke and a cigarette. But the house was silent during these prayer hours. I guess she was downstairs doing laundry. At the time, her not joining us, or leading us in prayer, never struck me as odd. Although we attended church as a family on holidays, and occasionally in short spurts during the year, in general, my parents didn't go to mass much.

On some Saturday evenings, my dad would go alone to church. I never wondered why he didn't take any of us kids with him. But then, sometimes when he and mom were not getting along, he would also go alone to movies. A few times, he even just went to the driveway and sat in his car. I think maybe during that period he was too tired to even drive anywhere for a little alone time. I guess if it didn't drain his battery, he would have stayed out there longer listening to music from a happier time for him. Maybe he was out there praying.

During the Good Friday hours of penance, I was supposed to be focusing on Jesus' suffering for my soul. But as the hours seemed to grow longer, I became captivated by the abstract concept of my soul. *What was it?* I wondered. *And what was so wrong with it that God had to send His Son to suffer so horrifically to save it?* Over the years, my intrigue led to mental exploration. When I reached my teens, I found my thoughts quite sacrilegious, and even charred with coals of confused anger. *If God is God, and Jesus was the Son of God in the flesh, couldn't they have come up with a better plan to reveal the importance of the salvation of all souls than a violent and torturous crucifixion?* That act alone seemed to give power to the very basest of human behavior.

I didn't come up with any answers, but the questions intrigued me.

Over the years, Mom let us ease up on our commitment to Jesus during the three hours on Good Friday. By those years, I didn't feel such reverence for that time of penitent prayer. Some of my frustration came from not being so willing to believe everything my mother said. For example, she told us all good people spent this time in prayer. *Aren't you a good person, then?* I wondered. But she was an adult, and in my parents' world, rules for kids and rules for adults seldom overlapped. What was she doing during noon and three? Better still, why were we kids so gullible as to keep praying while she was out of the room, and usually in another part of the house where she wouldn't be able to tell right away when we stopped or left?

I don't know why we weren't tempted to simply get off our knees and ask her these questions. Maybe Judy and Randy eventually did. But as a child I didn't question my mother or confront her about inconsistencies in her theory about what bad people did, and why I never saw God punishing them.

One Good Friday, in the silence of prayer time, I could hear the neighbor children laughing and playing outside because it was Friday and we had a day off from school. Some of these children were Catholic and attended our church, St. Linus. Why did they not know these Rules of Goodness or the punishable sins that my mother talked about with an expression of having just licked battery acid?

I knew the neighborhood children. We played with them all the time. My mother let us. Why would she if, according to The Gospels of Mom, they were such sinners? I listened for clues about my mother's theories. The best I could determine was that the neighbor kids weren't bad, necessarily, but they weren't being raised by parents quite as conscientious as my father and mother.

The same concept of people deserving punishment occurred on another Good Friday when, between 12:00 and 3:00, we could hear car horns honking excitedly. In the area where I grew up, weddings and receptions were always in two different locations—usually a church and then a VFW hall. At the time, it was customary for someone to decorate the wedding parties' automobiles with flowers made of bathroom tissues, white streamers, and maybe even tin cans tied with long strings so they tumbled and rattled behind them through the streets. Creative people added signs that said more than simply "Just Married." When my mom and dad wed, their sign read, "When cupid hits his mark, he usually Mrs. it." As these cars drove through the streets from one venue to another, they honked their horns, and people would stop to offer them a congratulatory wave.

I didn't know anyone married so early in the day, but that one Good Friday, a caravan of wedding celebrants broke the silence of our prayers with energetic, joyful honking.

"They're going to burn in Hell," my mother told us.

No wonder I never saw the horrid punishments my mother alluded to whenever anyone misbehaved. Apparently torturous penance from God was reserved for after death.

Over the years I felt my attitude slipping me closer to those pits of anguish. As we grew up some, Judy and Randy stopped praying on Good Friday, leaving Ray and me to do the praying for all of us. By these years, Mom eased up even more on her strict adherence to the "on our knees from 12 to 3" rule. One time, after an hour of having us pray at home, Mom took us to church to pray. I guess I was developing preteen rebellion because in response I thought, *Good, that'll kill a little time.*

St. Linus was silent. It wasn't packed, but there were plenty of people there walking the Stations of the Cross along the side aisles or kneeling in pews praying or saying their rosaries. At around 2:00, the priest showed up. He didn't say a whole mass (*Thank God*, I sighed), but he offered a blessing, and then splashed holy water at us. Mom seemed satisfied. When we left, although 50 minutes remained of Jesus' hours of suffering, we didn't have to pray in the car. But to acknowledge those hours, Mom didn't turn on the radio.

Playing music and singing during those hours were taboo. In my early teens, I tested the extent to which I could resume my usual activities during those three Good Friday hours. Judy and Randy had both pitched in money to buy the Broadway soundtrack to *Jesus Christ Superstar*. It was a brown, double-album (<u>*double!*</u>—*that must have cost them*, I marveled at their wealth) with a gold emblem of what looked like a horseshoe insignia formed by angels. I loved that album mostly because listening to it made me feel very grown up. One Friday evening when Judy went on a date, she let me sit in her room and listen to the whole album. I turned off the overhead lights and clicked on a cylindrical plastic lamp that flashed different colors that she had made in Junior Achievement. Then I started her turntable and listened to the album enough times to memorize some of the songs.

Good Friday of 1972, I headed to the basement pantry to get a can of vegetables Mom wanted (during Lent, we didn't eat meat on Fridays). As I ascended the stairs singing "I Don't Know How to Love Him," Mom reminded me that, even though we weren't spending this entire time praying, we couldn't sing between 12 and 3.

"But it's from *Jesus Christ Superstar*," I told her. "The whole story takes place during Holy Week." I knew parents who railed against the musical as blasphemous. I had a distant relative who would have fainted if she knew we had the album in our house. Though well-meaning during her visits, she would look through Judy and Randy's rock and roll albums and then question my parents like Columbo about why they would let their children listen to songs like "Maggie Mae" and "Aqualung." I'm sure my mother had no idea those songs were about an aging woman sleeping with a much younger man and about a grimy pedophile (maybe this relative had a point?), but Mom would not have her parenting questioned—by ANYONE, well-meaning or not.

So all Good Friday that year Mom let me sing every lyric I knew from *Jesus Christ Superstar*. During some of the songs I did think about Jesus and wonder about the passion and suffering. But honestly, it was such a relief being able to spend those hours off my knees and out of silence that mostly I just sang because I finally could. At the time, I didn't know that my singing days were over.

7

Depressed, Not Lazy

The descent into the dark night of my soul began at age 11. Though they came innately, I started making poor choices and developing negative perceptions—of others, and especially myself. Sometime during the return to St. Linus to start sixth grade I experienced the first shifts of puberty. Certainly that impacted the change in my personality. But it was a facet of the shift, not the catalyst for it. Something deeper in my self-perception had been developing since my earliest awareness, and new middle school challenges started bringing them to light.

I always enjoyed the company of females more than males. At family gatherings, I was allowed to congregate in the kitchen with my mother and aunts so long as I didn't intrude. In jaw-dropping awe, I never said a word. In the living room, the men argued politics and sports, spouting policies and statistics and names I never heard before. But in the kitchen, the women mixed and served Polish dishes like golompki and pierogis almost as delicious as their conversation. Mostly they complained about their husbands or gossiped about my aunt in prison. A movie buff since my youngest years, I often watched adult dramas, like *Cat on a Hot Tin Roof* on The Weekday Afternoon Movie. Tennessee Williams could have gotten some story mileage from the women in my family.

From infancy, I loved my mother more than anyone in the world. Throughout my childhood, I loved women in general. Though I couldn't articulate exactly what it was, I sensed a magical energy among women when there were no men around. Something kinetic seemed to make their interactions lively and exciting, captivating and vibrant. I never sensed that among my adult male relatives. I got the impression from the women in my family that they never did either. The most generous comment I ever heard a female relative make about the opposite sex came from a great aunt who once said of her brother-in-law, "He's all right . . . for a man."

Being allowed to sit among the women at family gatherings made me feel special and included. I was never confused about my gender identity. I knew I was a boy and never wanted to be a woman. But nothing made me happier than feeling this magic that only women seemed to create. That energy was feminine, and I liked it. But as a well-trained boy, I knew never to express it through comments or mannerisms that would be unbecoming of a male.

Among the nine households around our cul-de-sac, girls handily outnumbered boys, especially among children my age. Lucky for me, I loved playing with girls. Given a choice between adapting my tastes to do what girls wanted or other boys preferred, I would opt for the girls every time. I'd rather play house with Cathy and Jackie Farchione than tell nasty stories with the boys in Bobby Lake's secret clubhouse decorated with *Playboy* centerfolds he'd stolen from his dad's stash of magazines. In school, I played with both boys and girls, but found girls easier to talk to. Until the sixth grade, I was proud of myself for being ahead of my male peers at relating to girls. But in sixth grade the truth of my sexuality became clear to me. It jolted me so much, I could only take it in secretly.

From kindergarten through fifth grade, I was a model student. It wasn't enough to excel academically. Like my sister, I loved expressing affection for my teachers by being a helper. Because of the timing of our introduction, I felt no such compunction for Sister James Marie, who taught me history and religion. When I first entered her class, I was in an unusual attitude. I returned to St. Linus in sixth grade no longer planning to perpetuate the close bond with my peers or earn the admiration of my teachers. Mortified by the realization that I would never be a traditional adult male, I wished only to be invisible. This early reflex to disappear initiated my first contentious relationship with any adult.

From my youthful perspective, Sister James Marie was intimidatingly tall. She had a large forehead exaggerated by a curly brown pouf of hair protruding from a white-rimmed veil common to nuns in the 1970s.

That first week of class, my mother took me to buy school supplies at K-Mart. In the aisle choosing what color spiral tablet I wanted, I looked up to see that pouf of brown hair and four-star general forehead from the next aisle. Our eyes met. She didn't smile. I don't know if I decided before that moment that I was afraid of her, but I remember feeling as though our gaze locked for a piercing second before I turned, green spiral in hand, and joined my mother in another section of the store.

Any other year, I would have said, "Hello, Sister," or acknowledged her with at least a smile. But I felt too awful about myself at the time to muster the special courage it took me to interact with adults outside of my family. My dad had taught us boys how to shake hands firmly and look adults squarely in the eyes. When confronted with an opportunity like this one with Sister James Marie, I could have focused on the ritual and not been so intimidated. But that afternoon, I felt vapid and afraid. So, disrespectfully, I walked away from her.

Once out of her view, I thought about going back to greet her. The emptiness inside me filled with anxiety. I knew it would have been the smart action to take. She would be my teacher for an entire school year. While still in the store, I had one small opportunity to reverse the negative impression I must have made. The stirring anxiety could have given me enough adrenaline to propel me back to the school supplies section. I knew being polite and acknowledging her was the right thing to do. My parents had taught me well. But for the first time I felt a heaviness of self-doubt that dulled any spark of energy to move me away from my mother and back to Sister James Marie.

We never crossed paths again that afternoon at K-Mart. When my mother and I rode out of the parking lot, I didn't look out the window in case Sister saw me leaving without having given her the respect of a simple acknowledgment. My chance for atonement had passed. I started sixth grade feeling shy and self-conscious. I went to school the next day engulfed in dread.

When I encountered Sister James Marie at school the next morning, I sensed a coldness from her that confirmed how badly I had handled our awkward non-interaction. With one final childlike glimmer, I wondered if I might still repair the damage I'd caused. I did still care. But that hopeful spark fizzled. I didn't understand my new indifference.

Judy, my sister five years older than I, had grown sullen as a preteen. My older brother Randy was always quiet. When he had reached my current age, he simply faded from our family gatherings. I was so different from both of them, I couldn't imagine such a pall overpowering me. But in response to Sister James Marie, it did. I became immobilized by my own fear of opening up to another person. Rather than repair the damage, I responded to her coldness by matching it. I was in new and frightening emotional territory. But already it weighed so heavily on me I couldn't overcome it.

The new attitude changed my perspective. Once I was naturally happy and optimistic. Now I fixated on her actions that reinforced my decision to remain withdrawn.

One of Sister James Marie's religion lessons began with students taking turns reading an excerpt from The Bible. When one student read about Mary riding into town on her ass, Ed Jurkiewicz peered at his friend Dave Kosinski and giggled. Ed's response made Dave snicker. After a lingering, disdainful glance at Ed and then Dave, Sister James Marie turned to the class and growled, "Babies. I'm teaching a pack of babies."

In my better days, I would have known she wasn't referring to me. Born an old soul, I never indulged in silly shenanigans of boys my age. But her leer gave an image to the self-loathing I had adopted that school year, and I let her snide remark darken the rest of my day.

During a class session later that school year, she brought in a guest speaker, a priest from another parish. I was too young to realize at the time that she wanted to make a good impression on him, or that she had loaded her question with expectations that she would dazzle this priest with her teaching aplomb. Rather than merely introduce the priest and let him teach the class, she began by asking us, "Where is God?"

Dave Kosinski raised his hand. Dave—the one who had snickered with Ed Jurkiewicz about Mary's biblical ass—was tall and stocky and had already begun to transition out of the awkwardness that would define most of the rest of us until our mid-teens. Students liked him. Teachers liked him. I don't know if Sister James Marie liked him before his answer. "In the sky."

She winced as though stabbed. With a grimace, she echoed in disdain, "In the sky." Lips pursed, she retreated to the back of the room mumbling, "Babies." She echoed the sentiment as if we had learned nothing from her all the months she'd been teaching us. "Bunch of babies." I don't remember a single point the guest priest made that day. I only felt Sister James Marie's eyes crawling venomously across my neck.

My emotional withdrawal affected my attention and motivation. I didn't care about studying. I used to thrill at learning something new. Now I couldn't muster enthusiasm for much of anything. My young mind couldn't identify my current state as depression. I only knew that I felt indifferent to school and achievement. I had never before experienced a sense of oblivion, but nothing mattered. I take that back. Very little regarding school mattered or seemed memorable. But my mind latched onto every defeating incident. Somehow, they all starred Sister James Marie.

In the previous school years, I simmered in a pot of anxiety about missing anything important that I might need to know. From first grade, whatever a teacher said, I listened to intently. What a relief it was to learn to write. I began printing out anything they said I needed to remember. Most of it was information for tests. But other bits of information turned up the heat of that simmering pot.

"Remember to get your paper signed." It was customary to take our current classwork home to our parents to keep them apprised of our progress. I often filled the assignment sheet at the front of my green notebook with more information than the notes I took during class lectures.

In sixth grade, my assignment sheet grew more and more sparse. By mid-semester, I didn't bother to write anything. Test days came as a surprise to me. I'd enter class having no idea, or interest in, what we were about to do. I was so catatonic I didn't even sense the other students' anxiety about the major exams that apparently began shaping our future—or at least our chance to be accepted into a Catholic high school instead of being relegated to the drug-infested public junior high the nuns warned us not even to pass on our way home from school.

Days after our tests, the teachers would call us to their desk and hand us our graded exam with a pointed comment. After five years of praise, even I was surprised how numb I felt when the feedback, loud enough for everyone to hear, was meant to shame me back into my old, disciplined ways. One time Sister James Marie barked, "Leslie." I stepped up to her desk. I assumed I had done badly but was so disconnected from my own self-awareness I approached her without bracing myself for humiliation. "When you gonna hit the books, Leslie?" was an early comment. Over time, my grades remained so dismal they dragged the class's bell curve right off its axis. I became so oblivious to my own failure, it barely fazed me when Sister James Marie renamed me later by changing the statement to, "When you gonna hit the books, Lazy?"

There is a blessing in depression. I was too dead inside to even cry, which is what I would have done in years past. Thank God. To get misty-eyed in front of my peers, in the sixth grade, might have been unrecoverable. But I think my lack of response only fueled Sister James Marie's frustration. Others cowered at her roar. She must have interpreted my silence as an indifferent shrug. By the end of the first semester, our discord seemed all that bonded us together.

Throughout the year my numbing fog thickened. Until one incident with Sister James Marie, I hadn't even noticed how my mind had surrendered to a cozy haze of oblivion during class. One day before recess, Sister James Marie gave some instructions. I didn't realize I'd missed them until I felt a circuit of attentiveness among my classmates. She had apparently given some new rule I missed. In my mental haze, I didn't ask her or any classmate to repeat it.

It was spring, so after lunch we all had to spend 30 minutes outside. Most students played kickball on the parking lot punctuated by the school, convent, and rectory. I never played kickball, but I had a few incidents when I was featured in a game anyway. Usually, my friend Steve Hideg and I walked around and talked—me about movies and TV shows I watched, he about being in the band (he played trumpet like his older brother, Laszlo). Whenever we walked too close to a kickball game, invariably I would get beaned in the head. No one ever did it intentionally. Something fateful about me and sports ensured that I would be humiliated by them if I was anywhere near an event. To avoid the game (and mortification), I always steered our walk as far from the kickball activity as possible. That day I led Steve up the drive between the church and convent.

"I don't think we're supposed to go here anymore."

I didn't know what he was talking about. We always took this route. I just kept walking until we were parallel to the church entrance.

"I think Sister James Marie said—"

As if mentioning her name summoned her, a passing car slowed. Staring from the passenger seat was Sister James Marie. We didn't reenact the K-Mart eye-lock that still haunted me, but I glimpsed inside the car long enough to see a big forehead and brown loofah sponge of hair. In a gesture of silliness, I ducked behind the nearest pillar at the entrance of the church, pressing myself against the yellow bricks like a spy. I felt giddy, a young Maxwell Smart hoping Steve enjoyed my comic instinct.

Once the car passed, Steve, pale as the mortar between those bricks, warned, "We're in for it."

Until his reply, I honestly didn't know I had done anything wrong. Then something in my brain recaptured the seconds following the fog I had been in before lunch. So that's the announcement I'd missed.

At St. Linus, everything happened in perfect order. After lunch, all students lined up to go back inside by forming straight lines, divided by class, and then gender. At our entrance, it was sixth grade, then seventh, then eighth, always girls first, boys after. Our entrance doors led into a large foyer through which sixth graders walked directly to their hall on the first floor. Seventh and eighth graders turned left at the center of the foyer to ascend the stairs to their wings.

When Steve and I entered the foyer, Sister James Marie was waiting, dead center. Her eyes lasered into us. "Over here," she barked. "Now!"

Steve and I obeyed. Steve began immediately, "I'm sorry, Sister, I didn't—"

Without taking her eyes off me, she grasped Steve's shoulder. "Go to class," she directed him. Meantime, all the sixth graders shuffled past. The girls, a peripheral blur of burgundy plaid uniforms, sidestepped around us. Then the boys, their white shirts pungent with pubescent sweat and springtime, trailed next. I sensed their rubbernecking, and heard rumblings, but every comment remained indistinguishable under the cymbal crash of fear I felt locking eyes with Sister James Marie.

Right there in front of everybody—throughout my funeral procession of sixth and seventh and eighth graders—she reamed me out. "What were you doing there when I expressly told you NOT to go down that drive just a few minutes before?"

Of course, I had no answer. By walking to that area, I really wasn't being deliberately disobedient. I hadn't heard her instructions. I knew that was no defense. And if I did try to offer it, even I, at age 11, knew that my act of silliness—hiding behind the pillar as the car passed—made any argument entirely unbelievable.

Luckily it was a rhetorical question. She used it only to embark on a tirade that lasted until the last class of eighth graders snaked through the doors and toward the stairs. She ended with "Get away from me." I interrupted the line of eighth grade boys to reach my hall and classroom. Until this incident, I knew Sister James Marie was frustrated with my lack of academic effort. After it, I decided Sister James Marie hated me. And so did I.

Though I survived sixth grade, I spent the first week of summer vacation in dread. Any day our report cards would arrive in the mail, and my dad would hold in his hand evidence proving Sister James Marie right: I was lazy. But I was not dumb. When Dad called me into his basement office to "discuss" with me my report card, one argument came to me in the moment that saved me. I was born asthmatic, and that spring I missed two weeks of school because of the severest attack I'd ever suffered.

Especially at his angriest, Dad acted cool and deliberate. So he calmly confirmed that he thought my grades were inexcusable. I couldn't defend them. My report card could have guest starred on an episode of *Sesame Street* dedicated to the letter D. Then Dad asked me, in the same tone he questioned colleagues who discussed work issues from his home office telephone, what happened.

I told him being out of school sick those two weeks put me so far behind I didn't know how to catch up. So I gave up.

"Did you ask your teacher for help?"

I thought, *Sister James Marie? She hates me.*

I replied, "No, sir."

"Why didn't you ask any of us for help?"

As I shrugged an "I don't know," my mind flashed the true answer. *I hate me*.

My dad didn't punish me for barely passing sixth grade. Instead, he told me I *would* reestablish my A average next year, "or else."

I pictured the scary, long-haired kids who didn't wear uniforms at Haston Junior High. Despite the fear of becoming their classmate, I felt empty. I didn't know how I'd find enough resolve to raise my grades again. I had the summer to figure it out.

Unable to discover a solution on my own, I would stare into the clear summer sky seeking guidance from God. Then I'd remember Sister James Marie's response to Dave Kosinski. God was not there.

Then where? I wondered.

8

Hiding

Withdrawing further from the world, I spent most of that summer watching television. Paul Lynde's sweaty quiver in the center Hollywood Square made me feel sympathy for him. That's how I imagined I must have looked to Sister James Marie in the foyer. Yet anxiety intensified the delivery of Lynde's punchlines, most of which went over my head.

PETER MARSHALL: Nathan Hale, one of the heroes of the American Revolution, was hung. Why?
PAUL LYNDE: Heredity!

I didn't get it.

Other jokes resonated too closely for my developing self-awareness.

PETER MARSHALL: In *The Wizard of Oz*, the lion wanted courage and the tin man wanted a heart. What did the scarecrow want?

PAUL LYNDE: He wanted the tin man to notice him.

I did get that one and was offended. I loved *The Wizard of Oz*. When CBS broadcast it on their special Sunday night movie feature every February, Judy and I never missed it. What Lynde suggested about the scarecrow, one of my favorite characters, embarrassed me. From my narrow, Pleasant Valley Sunday view of the world, I had no idea Paul Lynde was gay. Instead, his joke suggested that he was making fun of such behavior. I read into it judgment. The peals of laughter reinforced in my mind the shame of my noticing men with curiosity and longing. I perceived the audience response as ridicule. My interpretations of the joke and reaction made me want to withdraw even more.

My lifelong fondness for girls and indifference to the interests of most boys confirmed what used to linger as a quiet backdrop of self-doubt. I began to feel certain what secretly attracted me and what didn't. That clarity made feminine qualities in men distasteful. Clifton Webb as persnickety Mr. Belvedere in the movie *Sitting Pretty* left me rooting for the sloppy toddler in the breakfast scene. He made me doubt my own masculinity and reinterpret how I might be coming across to others. I recalled my leap behind the pillar as Sister James Marie rode by. Instead of imagining me as Don Adams' Agent 86, I pictured my reflexive leap as more feminine, something befitting Charles Nelson Reilly. That summer I quit watching *Get Smart*, and I couldn't make it through a rerun of *The Ghost & Mrs. Muir*.

When I received my seventh-grade schedule, I was elated. No Sister James Marie anywhere. Sister Lidwina would teach me math. My older siblings had her for algebra. I'd have Sister Clement Marie for English. My siblings had liked their English teacher, Sister Clementisima. The similarity of the beginning of her name didn't tip me off as it should have.

History... History. I traced my finger down the course roster. Sister Ellen Maria. *What a pretty name*. So much more feminine, and less German novelist than James Marie. I liked her already. Something about her name comforted me. I didn't look forward to starting my next school year, but free of my nemesis, I believed I could survive.

The new school year brought some unexpected changes. According to explanations from my homeroom teacher, Sister Lidwina, the Pope or the bishop or the local diocese (I didn't know which—stepping back into a classroom regenerated the mental fog that got me in so much trouble the year before) loosened restrictions for the clergy. Most noticeable were the sisters' habits. They were shorter now, some up to their knees, and many wore white instead of the traditional brown.

In English class we learned that nuns could also change their names if they chose. Over the summer, many had picked new identities . . . something about re-clarifying who they were in the eyes of God. That teacher, Sister Clement Marie, was Sister Clementisima who had taught Judy and Randy. My underdeveloped middle school brain didn't recognize the clue that other familiar nuns might have changed their names, too. So all morning and lunch hour I felt comforted by relief. I could start this school year fresh because Sister James Marie really was in my past. I hadn't even seen her on campus yet. Maybe she went to another school, or better still, joined Mother Teresa in Calcutta.

I felt giddy reentering the school after recess. For the first time, instead of marching straight through the foyer, my class turned and ascended the stairs, a privilege reserved for the milestone of reaching seventh grade. In the metal name slot above the door to Room 202, printed in bold red magic marker, I read Sr. Ellen Maria. *Maria*. Sweet like Maria in *West Side Story*. Kind and child-adoring like Maria in *The Sound of Music*. (She was almost a nun, too!) Oh, I hoped. How I hoped.

I stepped into the room. Beyond the students who had taken a seat or were still clustered together, I saw a nun's back, crouched low at the bottom drawer of her file cabinet. She was wearing one of the new white habits. *This could be good.* Then she stood. Lean, towering, strong, with a pouf of brown like a large hairy turd on her forehead. It was Sister James Marie.

She didn't see me yet. I jumped back into the hall to recheck the name above the door. The gesture was quick but awkward. Worst of all, it reminded me of the silly, effeminate leap behind the pillar by the church. The sign indeed read, "Sr. Ellen Maria."

I trudged back into her classroom. I was already too defeated to even feel scared. Fear suggests at least a modicum of hope of some different outcome. There's energy in fear—the chance of fight or escape. I had neither. My seventh-grade year was doomed.

With my head and heart melted like candlewax, I never looked up to note Sister Ellen Marie's expression when she first saw me. It probably wasn't a surprise. She likely had scanned her new school year rosters hoping beyond hope that that lazy pain-in-the-ass Roger Leslie was not on hers this time. I was. She surely already knew it. Our first weeks that year were as cold and uneventful as an undiscovered corpse under ice-sheathed Lake Huron.

Even then, when pushed hard enough, I could be willful. When I was eight, my father signed me up for T-ball despite my protests. He asked me to at least give it a try. I tried to learn—for one practice. Fortunately, the coaches saw that my disinterest in the game matched my athletic ineptitude, so they gladly kept me out of play almost as much as I would have liked—which would have been completely. Kinloch Park, where the St. Linus Mavericks practiced and competed, was about four blocks from a street called Whitefield. With relish, I often told my female relatives that instead of having me play right field, the coach told me to just go to Whitefield and return after the last inning. I loved making my female relatives laugh!

But avoiding play did not come solely from the coach's compassion. I spent much of the season calculating ways to remain on the bench. One time, while dreading being the next up to bat, I watched the player ahead of me strike out—in T-ball. With earnest, he tried to hit the ball off the tee. The first time he swung with such fury his bat passed over the ball. As he spun into an embarrassed tumble at the plate, the ball, apparently caught by the wind of his zealous attempt, blew off the tee and plopped to the ground beside him.

Strike one.

In the moment, I totally missed my teammate's discouragement, so obvious to everyone else that even strangers in the crowd moaned and shouted encouragement. Instead, I felt the spark of inspiration for how I could stay out of the game.

Overwrought by his first strike, the player swung at the ball atop the tee twice more. The next two times he hit the tee, knocking the ball to the plate and striking out. The poor kid slunk away mortified while I took his place with clear resolve to repeat his folly. It worked, and in seconds I was back on the bench, this time sitting beside the boy, still tearful, as his father consoled him. I didn't try to feign remorse. But I pursed my lips to refrain from beaming.

Fall semester of seventh grade, Sister Ellen Maria reignited my willful resolve one day before the weekly church service that began our Friday school sessions. The church had purchased new books containing the order of mass and hymns. They were thick, small red binders shipped to the school in large boxes. In our usual orderly double lines, we students marched through the hall that connected the school and church. Each student received a red binder as we filed past Sister Lidwina at one line or Sister Clement Marie at the other. The system was effective. The lines moved as steadily as Charlie Chaplin squeezing through the cogs of his monstrous machine in *Modern Times*. Red binder in hand, I took my seat in church, the last student in the last pew of my class.

"Roger," Sister Mary Annett directed my attention to some old congregates seated at the back of the church awaiting the start of mass. "Get enough new books to pass out to them." She counted. "Eight. Get eight."

I waded upstream of the uniform flow of students still filing in. When I reached the foyer, Sister Ellen Maria was now the only nun passing out binders to both lines of students. When she saw me coming from the church, she snapped, "Figures. You *would* be the one not to follow procedure." She shot a book into my gut. "Now go. You've messed up the rhythm."

The shock of seeing Sister Ellen Maria and then being punched in the stomach with the hard plastic corner of the binder jolted me. Over the shuffle of student footsteps, I blurted, "It's not for me! *I HAVE MINE.* Sister Mary Annett sent me to get books for the old people in church."

I had never snapped at an adult before. I was raised to be respectful, especially to clergy. It was either "Yes, Father" or "No, Sister" or silence and downcast eyes. But now I was furious.

Sister Ellen Maria was stunned by my reaction. I don't know if the students went silent, too, but in my memory, the image of that moment remains soundless and frozen. The corners of Sister Ellen Maria's mouth curled in familiar disdain. She handed me the half-emptied box in front of her. "Here. Go back to church. You need it!"

I had nothing more to say to her in that moment. But I was shaken by the encounter. As I handed a binder to each old congregant, I felt the books slide wet with sweat from my trembling hand.

After that sniping exchange, I thought Sister Ellen Maria's iciness toward me thawed. But it was I who changed toward her. She didn't scare me anymore. My fear turned to fury. For several months, I wanted nothing to do with her because, instead of thinking of myself as a nothing in her eyes, now I thought nothing of her. Maybe my first instinct to avoid her at K-Mart was subconscious self-preservation. Throughout sixth grade, I gave her plenty of reasons not to like me. She was dissimilar to any other adult I'd known. The meanest ones I knew in childhood were some alcoholic great uncles. But they never threatened me; they simply ignored me.

My anger at her ignited a passion in my gut that suggested I actually had a backbone. Immaturely, I stockpiled negative impressions of her to feel superior. As she did every other Friday, Sister Ellen Maria gave us a chapter test. They weighed heavily on our grades, which were becoming especially important to students determined to get accepted in Catholic high school. The summer away from school did reignite my desire to excel academically, so once again I was studying for and doing well on tests. But nobody was as conscientious as Sandra Ferrera.

One of the few brown-skinned students in our community, Sandra was among the best students, and best human beings, in the class. Studious, respectful, diligent, she did everything right.

Because she had studied and would likely again get a perfect score on this chapter test, Sandra was the first student to finish the exam. She put away her pen, placed her completed test face down on her desk, and began reading the next chapter in the textbook.

A few moments later, Sister Ellen Maria leaned toward Sandra's row. "Is that a textbook open on your desk?"

Sandra was a timid and perfect child who never challenged an adult. So the sister's harsh question left her quaking. "Yes, Sister." Her quivering breath shook the words of her explanation. "Since I completed my test, I wanted to use my time wisely. I'm reading the next chapter."

Sister Ellen Maria barreled toward her. "You don't open your textbook in the middle of a test!" She snapped up Sandra's overturned test pages.

"But Sister!" Crescents of tears made Sandra's eyes glisten. "My pen . . . I put it away . . . I wasn't—!"

Sandra's protestations only added to the impact of Sister Ellen Maria's next move. She marched to the front corner of the room and flung Sandra's test into the garbage can. She turned to face, not Sandra, but the whole class. "Cheating is a sin."

"But Sister," Sandra repeated, this time in a whimper. The faith-killing horror of sweet Sandra's expression filled me with compassion for her. I wondered if someone as tender-hearted as a Sandra Ferrara would ever recover from such cruelty. The unfairness of the moment boiled within me. After the incident with the red binder and now this false accusation, I knew my anger was channeled appropriately.

The previous school year, I deserved Sister James Marie's disdain. I didn't greet her at K-Mart. I was her lazy student. She interpreted my silly *pas de chat* behind the church pillar as overt disobedience. That afternoon in the foyer, if she used me as an example of failure to teach some moral lesson to my classmates, I could now accept responsibility for inviting the inspiration in the first place. But Sandra Ferrara, an angel even through the awkwardness of middle school, deserved more respect.

Afterward, I stopped sandbagging all my experiences of Sister Ellen Maria like a self-righteous barricade in some Joseph Heller novel. I became more discerning. I could distinguish between when I was angry at her and when I was mad at myself. After expanding my perspective, my mind latched onto incidents with Sister Ellen Maria that contradicted my one-dimensional dismissal of her.

Although I had to rebuild my reputation as a conscientious student, I never wavered from my desire to be a good boy. Drilled into my mind throughout my childhood were Grandma Leslie's fervent instructions: Follow the rules. I liked rules because they supported my love of order and the safety of familiarity. Had my mind not been in such a fog last spring when Sister James Marie gave us the new rule about not roaming toward the front of the church, I never would have entered that newly forbidden zone. I wasn't rebellious. I wasn't even that adventurous.

But my fear of Sister James Marie had shifted to anger toward Sister Ellen Maria. Since the previous school year, I felt a stronger sense of self. Compassion for angelic Sandra Ferrara made me question Sister Ellen Maria's character. Though an impulsive reaction, I had snapped at Sister Ellen Maria for assuming I loused up her system by forgetting to take a red binder. I hadn't. I was being a good boy for Sister Mary Annette and for the older congregants without a binder.

Even at age 12, my desire to be good remained. For the first time, I sensed that being good was no longer prompted by my need for adult approval. Goodness was an ideal that made me think, somewhere in that boy I hated when I looked in a mirror, there actually must be some strength of character I could defend when it was unfairly challenged.

To my surprise, new observations of Sister Ellen Maria gave me new insights into her and myself. For an assignment one day in her religion class, Dave Kosinski had interpreted, phrase-by-phrase, The Lord's Prayer. I don't remember his exact translation. But I recall how impressed Sister Ellen Maria was with his efforts and insights.

"Did you do that yourself, David?" she asked in the most civil tone I ever remember her using with any student.

"My dad and I did it together," Dave confessed.

Sister Ellen Maria was temporarily speechless. But her palpable awe left me wondering what she would say next, rather than worrying that she was about to humiliate

Dave the same way she had Sandra Ferrara by telling him he cheated on the assignment by getting help from his dad.

"That's where God is. Not in the sky."

If her response weren't so melodic, I would have thought she brought up that previous incident to remind us what babies we still were.

"God is in your efforts to understand Him."

In that moment, all the self-protective techniques I had used to keep a psychological distance from Sister Ellen Maria dissolved. I saw something ethereal in her response to Dave. Everything in her kinesics—her open body posture, her contemplative eye contact, her compassionate tone of voice—made me temporarily feel safe in her presence. For this brief moment, as bright as the spotlight that I thought was God, I think God came through to me and let me feel a connection with Sister Ellen Maria my young mind had no way to anticipate. In that silent, temporary connection I witnessed between Sister Ellen Maria and Dave Kosinski, who would never again be included among her scorning "babies" assessment, I felt something palpable—the pure affection of respect. In the moment, I imagined the honorable peace that permeated the room must be what it felt to begin to know God.

Later in the year, another religion lesson from Sister Ellen Maria reached so far into me I caught a sad glimpse of my soul. The story was simple, and her delivery familiar. She led into the story scoffing about how other people do things wrong and fall short of their spiritual potential. This time it was not one of the "babies" she sneered about, but an adult. As her details unfolded, I wondered if she were insulting the parent of some other student in the room. I knew it wasn't one of my parents. They didn't even know Sister Ellen Maria.

The previous evening, Sister had a visit from a male layperson. After dinner, they strolled the sidewalk in front of the convent. Gesturing for Sister Ellen Maria to notice a male teenager with long red hair in the distance, the man snipped, "These young hippies will be the ruin of our entire world."

What Sister Ellen Maria told the class next surprised me. Instead of agreeing with the insult, she defended the young man. In a voice as tinny as usual, but tempered with a slow-simmering compassion, she told us, "This man was wrong. He didn't know the boy he was talking about. I do. He may have long hair, but he is a very religious boy. He even carries a little Bible with him wherever he goes. The man walking with me had no business saying that about a boy he didn't know." She paused, then made her point. "Don't judge people for one quality. We don't know who people are just by looking at them."

That moment proved enlightening for me. In that instant, I understood myself better. Who I had showed Sister James Marie I was last year revealed nothing of the truth of what was going on inside me. I appreciated how what I did (or, more accurately, didn't do) in her class last year made her think I was lazy. But I wasn't. I was sad and confused and ashamed that my sexual identity was a flaw that made me unlovable.

Despite the jaunty spring behind the pillar that Sister James Marie had mistaken for disobedience, I was still a rule follower. I had no intention of acting on my sexual desires because I never wanted to disappoint God. From that perspective, my new understanding didn't bolster my self-esteem. It only gave me a broader view of how endless and expansive was the dust bowl of my loveless future. From that vantage point I couldn't see God.

I felt helpless and hopeless, and thought I deserved to feel bad. I had started with every blessing a child should appreciate: a safe home, loving family, and caring adults committed to shaping my character. God gave me Paradise. I traded it, like thirty pieces of silver, for a wasteland.

Sister's comment about the Bible-carrying hippie reminded me that I was still seeking God. During that time, I spent many dead evenings walking our sweet dog, Bonnie, and asking God what was wrong with me. I was no hippie, but my behavior certainly invited judgment and misrepresented who I really was. Despite some obviously poor choices I was making to avoid embracing who I was, I still wanted my parents, my teachers, and God to love me.

Over time, my mental emphasis of Sister's story shifted. I stopped picturing a bald businessman in a suit making a judgmental comment to Sister Ellen Maria during their evening stroll. Instead, I envisioned that long-haired young man turning around and beaming, much like Jesus in some of the pictures in our catechism books—warm, light, kind. One of my first crushes was on this storied young man who loved God enough to carry a pocket Bible and was secure enough in himself to wear his hair however he wanted, no matter who judged him for it.

That crush changed my opinion of God, and of Sister Ellen Maria. She had defended that young man. I never imagined such compassion even resided in her heart. But it did. Further, she incorporated into her class lesson a personal story (until that moment, I'm not sure I knew nuns had personal stories) about being open-minded. To my surprise, I found this quality of Sister Ellen Maria very appealing. In her story, she modeled compassion.

That one insight opened my mind to perceiving Sister from a much broader perspective. Until then, I had her pegged: she was gruff, mean, and short-fused. But with a more open mind, I began noticing other facets to her.

In Michigan, spring teases multiple times before she arrives to stay. She'll bring warmth and sunshine, only to step aside for one more sleeting, or a powdering of snow that made the women's white Easter hats blend into the background of the outdoor photos families took after mass. Near the end of my seventh grade, spring finally burst with permanence in mid-April. We had all waited so long for sunshine and warmer weather. When only puddles of melted snow dappled the surrounding baseball diamonds, we children stampeded into the parking lot to play.

To our stunned delight, Sister Mary Annett, a tiny young woman with thick calves and a Mediterranean complexion, jumped onto a student's bike and raced toward Sister Ellen Maria, who had recess duty that day. Sister Mary

Annett remained upright as she pedaled, never dropping onto the banana seat, but leaned one way, then the other as she circled and swerved and sped through clusters of clapping students.

Giddy, Sister Ellen Maria raced after her on foot, waving one arm and shrieking in pursuit, pretending to try to stop her like a keystone cop. The tinny intonation that used to grate so threateningly now screeched with joy. Spring had opened her. Watching these nuns and seeing remnants of the girls they had been, I felt myself opening, too. I trusted my own intuitive joy. For me, the energy and innocence of that moment shed onto that scene the light of God.

For the last month she was my teacher, I felt drawn to Sister Ellen Maria. Even then I was an avid reader and movie lover. After that buoying observation of her in the parking lot, I started approaching her desk after class to tell her about a surprising plot twist of a novel I'd checked out of the library, or new information I'd learned about a favorite star from reading Rona Barrett.

I wanted to make peace with Sister Ellen Maria before I finished the school year, but I didn't know how. While standing at the door of my classroom waiting for the eighth graders to parade single file past us in the hall—girls first, boys right after—I saw a surprising exchange. As Sister Ellen Maria paced the hall watching the students leave, an eighth-grade boy grinned at her. "G'bye, gorgeous."

She wagged her finger at him, but playfully. "How you talk to a woman of God," she smiled, clearly delighted by the attention.

When it was my turn to process out of the building, I thought of trying the same line. After two years of making poor impressions on her, I might change her perception of me with a single comment. Approaching her down the hall, I grew increasingly nervous. My book bag rattled from the twitch of my arm. My throat constricted before I tried to speak. When I reached Sister Ellen Maria, I couldn't get myself to say anything. "G'bye, gorgeous" didn't sound like me. It wasn't me. As soon as I was too far past her to say anything, I regretted my lack of courage. Moments later, I was relieved. From that eighth grader, who was cute with his tousled hair and squinting green eyes, the line was charming. Given our history, from me it would have seemed crude and disrespectful.

A nagging desire to set things right with Sister Ellen Maria stirred consistently enough in me to try another tact. In history class, she taught us about the financial toll World

War II had taken on Europe. I didn't relate so much to the general gist of her lecture, but her mentioning finances sparked something I *was* interested in. Only the previous week I had cut out of the newspaper an article about *The Poseidon Adventure* setting box office records for the year. I had seen the movie for the first time over the previous year's Christmas break and was obsessed with it ever since. I already would have glued that article in *The Poseidon Adventure* scrapbook I'd started, but it was too big to fit.

After class the next day, I showed her the article (covered in a plastic sheath so she wouldn't smudge the newspaper ink). "The article says it's the highest grossing movie this year." I was so excited about the topic, I just kept rattling on. "It came out in 1972. Counting just the box office receipts from that year, *The Godfather* is still ahead of it. But because *The Poseidon Adventure* premiered at the end of the year, new polls are counting its revenue from 1973, and it set all kinds of records!"

"Wow," Sister Ellen Maria indulged me by showing interest, "you know a lot about finances."

I didn't. But I wanted to learn everything there was to know about *The Poseidon Adventure*.

"I didn't see the movie."

"Oh, you have to!" That spring it had been rereleased for another successful run and was still showing at some cinemas.

"I see you reading the paperback between classes."

She noticed something personal and so valuable to me. I did carry the novel with me to every class. I was already reading it for the second time. "Paul Gallico got the idea for the story while a passenger on The Queen Mary. The opening scenes of the movie are filmed on that same ship!" My inflection made the parallel seem miraculous.

"That's nice. I'll have to see it."

I hurried to my next class victorious. I not only made a real connection with Sister Ellen Maria, but I also convinced somebody else to see my favorite movie.

For the next few days, I asked Sister Ellen Maria if she'd gone to see the movie yet. She hadn't. Eventually, I could tell I was becoming a pest. That was a common occurrence with me and adults. I would talk about something I loved until I noted a look of dread in their eyes whenever I approached. So, I stopped talking to her about *The Poseidon Adventure*.

By this time, I had started reading books adapted into movies starring *The Poseidon Adventure* cast members.

Shelley Winters had won an Oscar for *The Diary of Anne Frank*, so I read that one. Because it was set during the Holocaust, I found a connection to history I thought would interest Sister Ellen Maria.

Even though we'd moved onto more recent history in her class, I told Sister how much her World War II lessons came to mind while I was reading Anne Frank's diary. I think my comment made an impact. She seemed pleased. I felt smart and informed relating details from the diary to lessons she'd taught. Clearly, I had paid attention in class. I had aced that chapter test. Now I was adding breadth to that learning by exploring it from another perspective.

"That's a wonderful book. So sad. How awful it must be to have to live in hiding."

Her comment jarred me. Was she implying something about me I thought only I knew?

Then she smiled. "I'm glad you're a reader, Roger."

My panic for what she might know dissolved in her compliment. Instead, I basked in her new reference to me. She called me Roger. Not Leslie. Not Lazy. *Roger*. I had risen above the shattering epithet. By earning my way back into her respect, I felt my self-esteem rise.

As a student, as a reader, as someone who had intelligence and study habits worth acknowledging, I felt a shred of self-respect and hope. If I could win over Sister Ellen Maria, maybe I could do the same with God.

One of the Greatest
Escape Adventures Ever

To disappoint God by what I did left room for atonement. But to incite God's disdain for who I was set my course toward Hell with no stop-offs in purgatory. I agonized, *How do I regain God's forgiving grace when there is no way to un-become who I have always been? If God made me, as both Baka and Grandma assured me whenever I asked (and I did ask, especially whenever I perceived myself as somehow gender unique), then why would acknowledging my true feelings make me automatically forsaken? That logic means I was doomed from birth. What kind of convoluted Creation story was that?* Even if I never acted on any of my feelings which, pre-puberty, had nothing to do with sexual desire and everything with hunger for love, I was blighted.

Realizing I was alone materialized in odd ways. One November, I heard Mom on the phone with Baka discussing the seating for a Thanksgiving dinner hosted by my Uncle Stan and his girlfriend Diane. To calculate how many folding chairs we would need to bring, Mom listed everybody who would be there. I listened to the roll call, and swore Mom skipped my name.

Later, Randy mentioned our family going to Stan's for Thanksgiving dinner.

"I didn't know I was invited."

Randy looked at me as if I were a strange, spoiled child. "What, you need a personalized invitation to family gatherings now?"

I didn't explain what prompted my comment. It seemed pretty stupid after I said it. But it hurt just the same.

My mind honed in on incidents that further separated me from my peers. In seventh grade, teachers stopped seating us alphabetically. Instead of sitting behind sarcastic Patti Kwatera or shy Kim Layman, I ended up sitting behind one of the prettiest girls in class. Mary Serwatowski was one of nine children. Her parents were involved in everything related to the church and school. Sometimes her mom set the milk cartons in the corner of each classroom before lunch. Other times she came to the classrooms during lunch to sell chips and pretzels. Mary's dad coached every sport for all her brothers. One cool spring Saturday while placing a ball on the tee for the next little batter, Mr. Serwatowski keeled over from a heart attack and died. The church community pitched in for tuition so that all nine Serwatowskis could have a Catholic school education at least through eighth grade.

Mary was one of the middle children. In fourth grade, she got the lead as Mrs. Santa Claus in the annual Christmas play. By sixth grade, her features suggested how pretty a woman she would become. Like many girls that year, she shortened the skirt of her uniform and began wearing makeup. I didn't notice any of that. In fact, I only realized that Marianne Matigian was the first to wear pantyhose because her thighs made a "swish, swish, swish" sound when they rubbed against each other as she walked.

At first, I made an effort to be friendly to Mary because I felt sorry for her about losing her dad. In time, I started enjoying talking to her and appreciated the attention she gave me. When I learned her birthday was approaching, I decided I'd buy her a gift.

"I want to get you something. What do you like?" I didn't know that most of my peers had already learned that by seventh grade boys and girls didn't just ask such blatant questions. They were more strategic so they could make an impression.

"I don't know. Surprise me."

I decided buying her a 45 RPM would fit my budget. I'd be willing to spring for a dollar gift for Mary. I just needed to think of a song that was age-appropriate. My tastes were not. I spent my early middle school grades listening to *The Partridge Family*, often indulging my loneliness touched by songs like "Doesn't Somebody Want to Be Wanted." Thanks to my love of movies and Academy Awards, I was by then listening to "The Morning After" and "The Way We Were," which my little brother Ray thought was a song for old ladies. Judy and Randy liked Led Zeppelin, Rod Stewart, and Bob Seger, who was from Detroit. I intended to buy Mary something in that rock and roll vein next time I was at Westland Mall. I never made it there before Mary turned 13.

What a relief I didn't get her the gift I had in mind. On the morning of her birthday, Dave Kosinski surprised her by leaving a little box wrapped in gold with a tiny silver ribbon on it. Before class, encircled by some of her best female friends, she opened the gift. It was a pair of gold friendship earrings.

Friendship earrings? I never heard of such a thing.

Mary and her friends were all impressed. Dave had suavely slipped back to his desk and was speaking to his buddies instead of staring her way to watch for her reaction. When Mary turned toward Dave, she had an allure in her eyes that looked so charmed, and so very adult. While her smile sparkled with a touching magnetism, Dave's close-lipped response was both shy and masterful. It was the first sexually mature interchange I had ever witnessed among my peers. I felt five years old.

Something more troubling occurred to me than my awareness of how far behind I was in maturity. I also knew that the reason I wanted to buy a gift for Mary contained none of the feelings that simmered in Dave and made him look handsome in his shyness. I didn't have feelings like that for Mary. I didn't feel that way for any girl. What concerned me more, however, was the realization that I related to what

Mary was feeling for Dave. I didn't feel that way for him myself. I didn't feel that way for any of my male classmates. But I did feel that way about one of a few high school teammates my brother Randy brought home to swim with him after football practice. These guys were four years older than I. What little time I spent with them was at my home, usually with my parents nearby. So, they were polite young gentlemen, a quality that has always left me surging with attraction. I didn't interact much with my brother's teammates. I assumed they perceived me as I saw myself—a nerdy, uninteresting kid. But somehow the contrast between what I felt around Randy's most handsome buddy and around my peers solidified in my mind that I was an outsider. What I liked and who I liked felt so taboo that I could only please God if I rejected that deepest part of me. If God could ever love me again, it would be only if I denied who I was and became an unnatural ideal I couldn't achieve.

That thought killed the possibility of staying in God's favor. As I interpreted my religion, it scorned my innermost desires of how and with whom I wanted to find love. It suggested I should not accept myself, or love as I naturally wanted. Even before my teens, I felt confused. In me, spirituality had formed its own trinity: God the Father who loved me unconditionally. God the Son, whose love was pure. God the Holy Spirit, whose passion somehow always stirred sensations that shaped who I was becoming as a man. That third element seemed at odds with the religion of my youth. The conflict sent me searching for faith where I could be loved by God for who I was—and always had been. As young as I was at the time, I sensed that if I were to survive this life, I might have to accept that there was something fundamentally wrong with me and settle for an unfulfilled life as one who could never find love. Without the prospect of love, life robbed me of all hope.

Stubborn as I could be, I refused to give up on the possibility of love. What life seemed to deprive me of personally, I sought vicariously through movies. At age 11, I was immediately captivated by *The Poseidon Adventure*, billed on the posters as "One of the Greatest Escape Adventures Ever." It was the escapism that first thrilled and distracted me from me. Two years later, I was almost as captivated by *Murder on the Orient Express*. Years later, some deep self-reflection revealed a parallel between the two films. I was enthralled by the concept of strangers being forced by natural phenomena and the direst of circumstances to connect with others to survive. In my teens, my lonely heart yearned for a circumstance that would force me from the isolation I had dug myself into so deep that I didn't know how to get out alone.

I didn't yet have the courage or understanding to know I could reach out to other people to find my way out of the depression into which I kept sinking deeper and deeper. Instead, I searched for spiritual answers by indulging in the escapism of religious movies. I became enthralled first by depictions of Jesus, and then more broadly and profoundly, spirituality in general. Although it didn't relieve the vacuity of loneliness, watching these movies and then exploring my reaction to them did give me clearer insights into myself. What I learned first worried me.

Watching religious movies blended a spiritual and psychosexual attraction to the character of Jesus. While watching *King of Kings*, for example, I felt humbled and confounded by the power of Jesus' ability to perform miracles. But mixed into that spiritual awakening was a dichotomous attraction to Jeffrey Hunter. Physically, I was aroused by his penetratingly handsome features. Emotionally, I hungered for a male as gentle and warm as Jesus to notice me, to love and hold and accept me exactly as I was . . . and exactly as I could not yet accept myself.

One Easter week, I went through the *TV Guide* and highlighted every religious film that would broadcast when I wasn't in school, and I watched every one. Most were variations of familiar stories. While watching *The Bible: In the Beginning*, I felt stirred by both John Huston's booming baritone as the voice of God and naked Michael Parks as Adam. I sat through *The Greatest Story Ever Told*, which ran so long it was divided into two parts on consecutive days of *The Afternoon Movie Showcase*. Already into studying movies and movie stars, I was less intrigued by the words of Jesus from Max Von Sydow's monotone delivery than by the frequent sudden cameos of famous stars with single lines of dialog. (Shelley Winters: *I'm cured. I'm cured!* John Wayne: *Truly, He is the son of God.*)

But the film that moved me most, perhaps because I could not be distracted by a handsome man in the scenes of spiritual revelation, was *The Song of Bernadette*. The opening sequence outside Lourdes when young Jennifer Jones encounters the ethereal vision of Linda Darnell as The Virgin Mary was stirring in a purer way than how I felt watching Michael Parks run nude through the Garden of Eden, even if on television I couldn't see anything arousing. Jones' expression, the lighting effects around Darnell, and the punctuating music brought me as close to what I imagined a true spiritual incarnation to be. The context was so much riper for me to hear the voice of God. Alone, propped on my elbows on the green living room carpeting in front of our color RCA console TV, I identified with the humble zeal depicted in Jones' innocent awe. I wanted to know God through sweet reverence.

Yet every church service the congregation had to confirm, "Lord, I am not worthy to receive you . . .." Being gay seemed the reason that line must be true for me.

10

Hope

Although my mother's half-brother Stan was the most independent person I knew as a child, he still lived with Baka in his twenties. Nevertheless, Stan lived by his own rhythms, keeping a schedule like no one else. I don't know what he did or where he went at night, but when we stayed overnight with Baka, my Uncle Stan could sleep like a corpse until noon. In fact, about that time of day, Baka would have Ray and me clamor, as loudly as possible, into his bedroom at the back of her house to wake him. Shaking Uncle Stan did no good. Climbing on top of him seldom helped. Baka handed us a huge red plastic blow horn to blast into his ear when every other attempt failed.

Even after the eardrum-bursting blare, he could still remain cemented face down on his pillow. Eventually he would stir, warn us in graveled fragments to get off him and keep that damn horn away from his head. Quite a while later, my uncle would shuffle bleary-eyed into the kitchen as we finished lunch. With afternoon sun beaming through Baka's kitchen curtains, Baka dropped our empty lunch dishes into the sink and got a skillet sizzling on the stove. "How 'bout fried eggs today, Stan?" she resumed cooking, knowing he wouldn't be coherent enough to reply to any question until after he ate.

Though he was not traditionally handsome, Uncle Stan could attract the most beautiful women. He had appealing features: large, dark eyes and curly hair so thick it was hard to tell the size of his head. His pronounced Adam's apple trembled when he laughed, and he laughed often because, once he was awake, he was very funny.

Uncle Stan's life was like his driving. After surviving one of his rollicking rides, Baka noted, "One lane ain't good enough for Stan." He was wild and erratic behind the wheel, but he treated everything very casually. When he was driving our car once, with Mom in the front seat and some of us kids in the back, he steered by manipulating the large leather-bound appendage protruding from the center of the steering wheel. When he tried to turn a corner, the big appendage came loose in his hand. As we careened, he remained totally calm. He extended the disconnected piece to my mother and asked, "Do you think we need this?"

"Stan!" my mother screamed, scared but amused.

Unfazed, he regained control of the car, reconnected the dislodged piece, and kept driving as if we hadn't almost crashed.

It might have been his sense of humor that attracted not only very beautiful, but often very serious women to him. Toni Dinda, his fair-skinned Italian girlfriend with the Twiggy haircut, came into our lives when I was only eight years old. She was so lovely, even I developed an inexplicable crush on her. Whenever she and Uncle Stan visited, I'd race to my bedroom and write her a love letter. During some of their visits, I'd give her just my letter. Other visits, I'd monopolize her attention showing her my school art projects and assignments that earned gold stars.

One time their visit was so short I returned with my freshly created ode to her only to discover they'd already left. I rushed back to my bedroom brokenhearted. My dad sat on the bed next to me and explained that I shouldn't write her notes or poems anymore—she was Uncle Stan's girlfriend, not mine. After Dad's talk, my infatuation with Toni tapered off. Soon I refocused on my most exciting goal that year—collecting every *Josie and the Pussycats* pencil eraser that came free in boxes of Super Sugar Crisp cereal.

From the time Uncle Stan received his draft notice until he left for Vietnam, Toni cried nonstop. My mother said Toni shed enough tears to fill our backyard swimming pool. The separation or the stress proved too much for Toni. His departure marked the end of their relationship.

Perhaps because as a cook in Vietnam he did not see active duty, Uncle Stan did not seem as scarred by the war as many others. But he returned more mature and attracted a different kind of woman. Diane Martinez was nothing like Toni in looks or personality. Whereas Toni was a dazzling showpiece who clung to his arm like a stylish sleeve, Diane wore little makeup and appeared to do no more than shampoo and brush her casually styled mane of black hair. Unlike Toni, Diane never reached for his hand as he conversed with others to ensure he still knew she sat beside him. Toni would stare at the knuckles she grasped, oblivious to anyone else in the room. Diane responded to Stan's inattentiveness to her by engaging in the group conversation.

It may have come down to a difference in tough life experiences. I don't recall any challenging details from Toni's life, but Diane had already faced tragedies. Her father, a roofer, crushed his skull when he slid off a three-story building. Mr. Martinez's fatal accident occurred several years before Baka invited Diane and her mother to a Christmas Eve dinner. In my short life, I had never met anyone so paralyzed by grief as Mrs. Martinez. All the features of her face sagged like a melting candle. Sitting beside her on the couch, I kept hearing what sounded like a dog growling in successive breaths. It was Mrs. Martinez, moaning with every exhale.

I thought she was sick. "Do you feel all right?"

"My husband died," she replied. I knew. Every time Diane introduced her to anyone visiting that day, instead of echoing the other person's "Hello," she told them, "My husband died."

"They know, Mom," Diane would stroke her mother's arm and walk away as if she couldn't bear hearing her mother repeat the same story again.

Later I heard Diane tell my mother in private, "I have a brother. My mother has two sisters even younger than she is."

I wondered how old Mrs. Martinez was. She had no gray in her hair, but her skin was blotched and sallow as a rusting tin can.

"But all the time it's me she needs. And everybody else tells me, 'You're so good with her.' I'm not," Diane confessed with the authority of a proclamation.

Her voice raised in anger, I think to keep herself from crying. "'Give her to Diane,' they say. 'She can handle her.' I can't." Another pounding declaration. The tears fell anyway. "I'm 23 and I'm already so tired."

"What does Stan say?" my mom asked.

Diane shrugged and walked away in defeat.

"Diane?" I heard Mrs. Martinez call from the living room.

I thought I'd help. "Can I get you something, Mrs. Martinez?"

Her mouth, always open and downturned, attempted a little smile. "You're a nice boy." She took one creaking breath then asked, "Do you know Jesus?"

Do I know Jesus? I didn't know what to say. No one had ever asked me. Like the most naïve of 12-year-olds, I said, "Yes."

"But you're Catholic?"

"Yes."

"Then you don't know Jesus."

I didn't have a clever retort.

"Did you come to the altar and give your heart to Jesus?"

During Holy Week, I always went to mass several times—for a service with my class, for Good Friday prayers between 12:00 and 3:00, and to get our Easter baskets blessed on Saturday. Sometimes we kissed the feet of Jesus on the crucifix statue laid at the altar for that purpose.

Give my heart? I didn't know what she meant.

"You can't be saved if you don't give your heart to Jesus."

Saved?

"You need to be saved or else you'll spend eternity in Hell."

Feeling cornered, I wished I could think of some wise but punctuating reply to ease my way out of this conversation. I held my tongue because all I thought to say was, *So, your husband's dead.* I stood. "I'm going to get myself some water. Want some?" The rest of that day, and every other time we met, I avoided her.

But I liked Diane. She never put on airs. Some adults I knew would use words like *amongst* in a context that, even as a kid, I could tell was only meant to make them sound smart to people they didn't know well. "I found the French cut green beans amongst the other canned goods," one of my aunts told a woman from church who belonged to the Bonnie Brook County Club.

But Diane was the opposite. The following Thanksgiving, Uncle Stan and Diane hosted their first holiday dinner in the one-bedroom apartment they rented. I didn't know where Mrs. Martinez lived, or if she lived alone like Baka and my other grandmother. But given what I'd heard Diane tell my mother the previous Christmas Eve, I wondered if Stan and Diane leased a one-bedroom to ensure that her mother couldn't tag along.

Clearly, preparing this meal was an experiment for Diane. She got no help from Stan or her mother who never moved from the couch until dinner was served.

At our house, my dad always did the honors of carving the Thanksgiving turkey. When he saw that Stan was not moving from the couch until he took his seat at the dinner table to be served, Dad stepped into their small kitchen and used the electric knife my parents brought to start carving. Having something to do probably helped take Dad's mind off the fact that he felt uncomfortable being in the apartment of a couple who was not yet married.

While Baka and my mom dug serving utensils and candles from the sacks they brought, Diane told us kids where on the table to place the different dishes she'd prepared. As Diane handed me a bowl of black olives, she asked my mother, "What exactly does 'pitted' mean, anyway?"

"It means they took the pits out."

"That doesn't make sense. If it says 'pitted,' I thought it meant it had pits. I didn't want that, so I bought the other kind. Then I opened the can this morning and they all have pits. I don't get it." She shrugged. "There's a lot I've gotta learn before Stan and I get married."

Dad perked up at that comment. "Married?!"

"Stan didn't tell you?"

"Stan," my mother called to him in the far corner of their living room. "You're getting married and you didn't tell us?"

He didn't reply. I think one of the Lions caught a pass just as my mom asked the question.

Mom turned to Baka. "Ma, did you know?"

"You don't think I woulda tol' you?"

"A wedding!" Mom beamed. In a brief silence between football plays on the television, I thought I heard Mrs. Martinez moan.

When my mother jumped on any bandwagon, she usually knocked everyone else off and took such tight grip on the reigns her blue veins pulsated over her knuckles. I don't know why Stan and Diane's wedding dulled over other thoughts or concerns she had throughout that winter, but it became her sole focus. Several reasons were possible. She may have taken charge because she was the oldest child wanting to plan the wedding of her youngest sibling. Perhaps she shared Dad's judgment about the unwed living conditions.

Ultimately, I think it had more to do with Diane and her mother. Diane's youthful innocence about cooking told Mom she would need plenty of help. Who would help? Baka, who was asthmatic and never much of a planner, wouldn't do it. That left Mrs. Martinez. The maudlin possibilities of Mrs. Martinez organizing a reception were certainly enough to turbocharge Mom into action. Mom was convinced Mrs. Martinez couldn't do much of anything useful because, as Mom said, she was "too eaten up with Jesus."

"I called St. Linus," Mom later told Diane over the phone. "They have a Saturday available March 17, if that's what you want. The local VFW hall is available for the reception that same day. I didn't want to chance losing either, so I scheduled both for you and Stan—if you feel comfortable with that. I didn't pay the deposit without talking to you, but I have the check written. That can be your wedding gift from Rick and me."

"Oh, Jerry!" Diane spoke my mother's name so loudly even I could hear her through Mom's receiver. "I don't know what's more generous—your gift or all this work you're doing. Thank you."

"So that's a yes?"

"Don't I need to talk to Stan?"

"Diane." Although Mom was on the phone, she was making that incredulous face when something was so obvious she thought you should be embarrassed to even ask. "It's Stan."

"I guess he won't mind."

A few days later, Mom invited Stan and Diane to dinner to compile the guest list. After we ate, Mom asked Stan and Diane to stay at the kitchen table I'd just cleared so they could make plans.

Stan stood and instructed Diane as if she were a child. "Whatever Jerry tells you is good with me. Just make sure we have an open bar and you invite my buddies from service." Stan headed toward the living room to join my dad.

Diane called to him, "Stan, I don't know your buddies' names or addresses."

"I'll get 'em to you," he called.

"When?"

"I'll get 'em."

Diane deflated the same way she did when her mother had become too much for her.

Mom's next comments didn't help. "I told you. But I guess you know better than anybody what you're getting into by marrying Stan."

When I finished washing the dishes, Mom had me join her and Diane to compose the guest list. From then on, I became Mom's wedding planner secretary. Because I loved my mom, and because I didn't know anything about weddings, I not only agreed with her every suggestion, but I praised it as if she had come up with something new and brilliant.

As if Christmas weren't even coming, my mother kept a peephole concentration on only the wedding. When

Mom learned that The Polka-tels, the most sought-after traditional Polish wedding band in all of Detroit, had had a cancelation for March 17, Mom raced to the bandleader's house to give him a deposit check. When I asked her if I should write that down, she told me I was her assistant, not her accountant. She would keep track of costs.

Throughout, Mom's tornadic planning so dazed Diane, she never objected to anything. In fact, she seldom even expressed a preference or concern. The first indication of her even having an opinion—or any say in what happened at her wedding—came when Diane started shopping for a wedding gown without my mom. Instead, she invited her own mother to the fitting. If Mom thought anything of being excluded, she never said.

By midwinter, the wedding plans were set. My Uncle Stan was willing to do what my mother said he had to. He agreed, and genuinely did not seem to have an opinion. When Mom scheduled a date for my dad to take Stan and his groomsmen for tuxedo fittings, Stan showed up on time. It was in the morning, and Stan needed no blaring horn or jumping nephews to get him up and out and where he was required to be.

Growing up in a Polish Catholic family, I knew only the traditions of my ancestry and religion. The Eastern European dishes—stuffed cabbage (golompki), dumplings packed with potato and cheese, or mushroom and sour kraut (perogi), were standard on holidays, and made weddings warm and familiar. Traditional wedding reception music included the "Tatusiu Waltz," which sent guests lining the parameter of the dancefloor to watch the bride have one final dance with her father. Stanzas, sung alternately in Polish and English, included lines such as "Don't be sad today, Daddy" and "I'll never forget you, Daddy" intended to bring everyone to tears before the music escalated to a polka for the Grand March where every guest paraded around the entire reception hall.

Because Diane's father was dead, she asked my mother if she could skip the waltz. Dancing it with her brother, who would have done the honors in the absence of their father, seemed too potentially sad to Diane. But the other traditions—the Grand March at midnight, and then leading the wedding party through another special dance where the bride passed her veil to her maid of honor and then each bridesmaid—intrigued and even excited Diane.

She lit up when Mom first told her that my dad would lead the Grand March and Mom herself would coordinate the passing of the veil.

Diane beamed, "This is all so new and interesting."

Her comment surprised me. I had never been to any other kind of wedding, so it didn't occur to me until then that different cultures—of which I had almost no personal experience, but was reading about in our geography textbook that school year—would have different traditions. I noted how Diane's ocher skin contrasted with my mother's pale Eastern European complexion. That's when it struck me. Diane was guided by my mother into having a Catholic ceremony, which included a full mass, and Polish reception. Diane's father was Mexican. Her mother was Italian. Although Diane knew Catholic traditions and had even been baptized because her father had been devout, I learned she practiced no faith after her father died. Mrs. Martinez went the other extreme and turned her life over to Jesus. Diane drove her to church twice a week—every Sunday morning and Wednesday evening—because Mrs. Martinez couldn't drive, but Diane never attended with her. "I'm not a happy-clappy, jump for Jesus Christian" was all the reason she gave.

It may have been only because most of the wedding plans were set by then, but we didn't see much of Diane and Stan until the week before the wedding. Realizing Diane probably didn't know how to polka, Mom invited the entire wedding party to our house for a dance rehearsal. We moved all the furniture against the walls of our basement, and Mom pulled out her slightly scratched *Music of a Polish Wedding* LP.

"We used this album to practice for our own wedding," Mom told Stan and Diane. Then she had us all watch as my dad and mom bobbed around the makeshift dancefloor to the accordion strains of Clare Witkowski and His Orchestra.

Pre-wedding excitement reached its zenith that night. Surrounded by Mom and Dad, Stan and Diane and all four adult couples from their wedding party, and Baka and my brother Ray and cousin Kim, the ring bearer and flower girl, I felt giddy. Baka didn't dance but observed and gave feedback. "Turn more, turn more," she told me while I practiced with Kim. The booming staccato music and whirling "hop-step-step" of the polkas accelerated as we found a rhythm and occasionally even mastered the steps for a full cycle around the basement floor.

When the lesson ended, Baka and Stan were seated on swivel chairs against the wall. Diane seemed as excited as I still felt. Prior to tonight, her face remained characteristically expressionless. She often breathed through her narrow mouth because her bottom lip usually hung open, a squared little purse like the lifted spout of a Morton's salt dispenser. Lit with excitement, her smile spread, the corners forming two optimistic arrows pointing to the sky. "That hop-step-step," she demonstrated as she spoke, "once I got it, it was pretty easy."

Watching her, Stan burst into a single, cruel "Ha!"

She stopped bobbing.

"You're not dancing. You're bouncing around like a rabbit on LSD."

The room went silent.

"Well, Stan," Diane held back tears. "I'm tryin'."

Long before he was drafted into the army, I couldn't get close to my uncle because he lived only in his generation, never interested in playing children's games with me. Even among adults, Stan always did what he wanted, when he wanted. I thought he was self-centered. But I never saw him be mean without a hint of humor. His "Ha!" was not funny. It was piercing.

I knew how it felt to be embarrassed in front of everyone in a room. I had made stupid comments in the past intending to be funny, only to watch eyes leer and roll. But Diane hadn't made a stupid comment. She was trying to learn something to fit in at her own wedding. Though I wasn't even a teenager yet, I wondered why my soon-to-be Aunt Diane would love somebody who could be so mean in front of the people closest to them.

Nothing more came of the comment. Nobody reprimanded Stan or came to Diane's defense. Not even me. I went to bed that night trying not to let that "Ha!" echo in my head and dampen the exhilaration I felt most of the night.

Mom's meticulous planning resulted in a grand success of a wedding. By March, decorations in St. Linus church were between the glittering reds and golds of winter and the pastel purples of Easter. For her blank canvas, Mom chose white flowers to burst with joy behind the pinks and burgundies of the bridesmaid's dresses. Traditionally, as mother of the groom, Baka wore a blue gown, her sheer long sleeves revealed only after she removed her wet overcoat and set it in the cry room where the bridesmaids awaited their cue to process toward the altar. Her white corsage, mounted on lace and sprinkled with babies breathe, matched the flowers on the altar. So did Diane's bouquet.

At the end of one pew, with my little cousin Barry on my lap, I watched the wedding party enter, two-by-two. The music changed. Everyone stood. Escorted by her brother, Diane stepped through the double doors of the foyer to process down the white carpet. I saw no tears of joy glistening through the veil. There was no smile—joyful or nervous—as she stepped, stiffly without the least hint of bobbing, toward Stan and Fr. Varison. She had reclaimed her usual expression, plain as salt.

By the time the bride and groom arrived for the reception, every rug in the foyer of VFW Post 7546 was soaked, umbrellas leaned against the wall, and coats dripped from the rack. The photographer caught Stan helping Diane off with her rain jacket after they entered. Semi-dry, they stepped into the hall where a stocky Polish caterer, her gray 'do flattened by a hairnet and a tray trembling in her pudgy hand, offered them a bite of bread, a dash of salt, and a sip of wine to symbolize a healthy, prosperous, and flavorful marriage.

Though she looked a little confused, Diane giggled with pleasure. My mother, standing with the caterer, told Diane, "Another Polish custom."

After dinner, guests encircled the dancefloor as the Polka-Tels invited Stan and Diane to take their first dance as husband and wife. Mom and Dad had taught them the waltz appropriate for this song, but they apparently forgot the lesson. Instead, they swayed in unison. Throughout the song, they spoke to each other.

"That's sweet," someone beside me said.

In reply, another guest grunted. It was Mrs. Martinez.

Not long after the wedding, Uncle Stan and Aunt Diane bought a house less than a mile from ours. My little brother Ray and I often rode our bikes to visit. As a postal carrier, Aunt Diane began and ended her workday very early. Uncle Stan was a pipefitter at the Ford Motor Company plant in Dearborn, so he was rarely home in the afternoons when Ray and I swung by for a cookie and some lemonade. Aunt Diane seemed tired a lot. Often when we visited, she sat in the backyard with a beer and her radio and watched us play with their shaggy black dog named Lovey.

I liked Aunt Diane. She was an adult who seemed to get along with anyone of any age. Once when she and Uncle

Stan came to visit, I was listening to *The Now Explosion*, a compilation album I'd purchased at Korvettes.

When Steely Dan's "Do It Again" started, her face lit up. "I love this song." The gleam in her smile reminded me that I hadn't seen her this happy since the dance rehearsal in our basement—before Uncle Stan laughed at her.

With Steely Dan's refrains still pumping, I felt my heart accelerate. I loved this song, too. It felt affirming to enjoy something an adult in my life also liked. It made me feel grown up because the phenomenon was rare. I was accustomed to being teased for having interests that my peers thought were nerdy (memorizing facts about U.S. Presidents in 3rd and 4th grade) or immature (the highlight of my 4th and 5th grade weekends was watching *The Brady Bunch* and *The Partridge Family* on Friday nights).

I didn't develop a crush on Aunt Diane as I had Toni Dinda. But our mutual love of that song made me feel even closer to Aunt Diane. As important to me, she was one of the few adults in my life, besides my parents and grandmothers, who seemed to like me.

Her animated response to "Do It Again" also made me think I could make her happy. Subsequently, every time she visited, I ran to my stereo and asked, "You want me to play Steely Dan for you?!" She indulged me the first few times. Then one afternoon, when I made the offer again even though she only stopped by to drop off something for my mother, she said, kindly but clearly, "You know, Rog, just because I like the song doesn't mean I need to hear it every time I come over."

I was stunned to curious silence. That hadn't occurred to me. When I liked something—a movie, a book, a song—I never grew tired of it. "Okay."

Diane sensed my confusion. "Next time you come over, bring your album. We'll play it then."

"Okay!" I liked that idea.

"Some of those songs are great party music."

I asked her if she would really ever invite me to a party.

"Of course," she replied. Throughout our extended family, children were never welcome at parties. When my parents hosted, we kids stayed with Baka, or Dad moved the black and white portable into our bedroom where we could watch TV until we fell asleep. I never believed Aunt Diane would really invite me to a party, but having just turned 13, I felt very mature when she said she'd include me.

During the same spring I repaired and redefined my relationship with Sister Ellen Maria, I thought the suggestion of an invitation from Aunt Diane brought adult acceptance. Naïve and unsuspecting of what life imminently had in store, I didn't know that the invitation I eventually accepted from Aunt Diane would crush my temporary elation into defeat.

11

Jesus Was a No-Show

Aunt Diane and Uncle Stan were only married a few months when a predawn phone call shocked us all awake. Dad got to the family phone in the kitchen first. It was Aunt Diane.

Like my dad, I'm alert early in the morning. I came into the kitchen, but Dad wasn't saying much, and I couldn't make out the voice on the other end.

"It's all right, Diane." Dad paused. Something about the timbre and delivery of Dad's instructions always comforted. I knew it worked with all us kids. But apparently it worked with adults, too. "I'll be right there," he assured. "Everything's under control."

Dad returned to their bedroom to tell Mom that Diane had been in an accident.

My mother's bleary reply struck me as odd. "Not in Stan's Camaro?!"

Dad was already getting dressed. "No. She was delivering mail. It was in that tiny mail truck."

That didn't seem to register with Mom.

"I'm going to check on her," he left Mom in bed.

"Dad, can I come?"

"No, son. I don't know how bad she is. I may need to take her to the hospital."

Hospital?

"Don't worry. She couldn't be too bad if she was able to get to a phone and call me."

Like Dad's unwavering tone, his logic comforted.

Only after Dad left did I wonder why Aunt Diane called Dad instead of Uncle Stan. Later that morning, Dad returned home with Aunt Diane. I never saw her in uniform before. She wore a light blue blouse with patches and knee-length shorts. It was midsummer and her calves were as tan as her arms and face.

But her expression was numbed by fear. With Mom and Dad seated at either end of the kitchen table, and my brother Ray and I opposite her, Aunt Diane retraced the details of the accident as she remembered them. When she spoke, her voice quivered as much as her limbs. She spoke so low, my mother snapped off the window unit air conditioner. In between details, I could hear Aunt Diane's stuttering breaths, and Mom's pencil scratching as she took notes to later share every grim detail with relatives.

Diane was driving her small postal truck through an intersection when a boxy Lincoln Continental plowed into the rear driver's side of her vehicle. Being hit from that angle probably saved her life. The collision threw the truck sidelong into a pole, dissecting that half of it, and stopping just before it crushed her.

"It's a miracle I wasn't killed." Diane wept.

Mom's reaction to the tears was electric. "You kids go on. Leave us adults alone."

We weren't allowed to see adults cry. Except for a great aunt who crumbled emotionally after losing her husband and son to heart attacks in the same year, I never saw an adult weep. My parents did not abide children crying either. If we did, they sent us away. My mother couldn't even stand hearing a baby cry in public. Although she'd never tell the parents to their face, she always growled under her breath, "Either feed it or beat it, but shut that kid up."

Aunt Diane didn't stop crying for some time. Even after she settled down and we all gathered around the table for lunch, Diane's tears started again when she retold the story to Randy and Judy. "It's a miracle I wasn't killed on the spot."

"Did you see your guardian angel?"

"What?" Diane stared expressionless at Judy.

"Baka says we all have a guardian angel."

"Saints are watching over us," my mother confirmed.

"No," replied Diane, still distracted. "It was bigger than that. The power that saved me must have been even greater." Then she mumbled something I had only heard from her mother. "Thank You, Jesus."

Diane was never the same after the accident. The changes were subtle at first. Her hair got longer. When her tan faded in autumn, her face looked unfamiliarly pale. She stopped wearing makeup. But the most apparent change emerged in her topics of conversation. She only talked about God.

As a boy whose sole exposure to religion was the Catholic mass, it took me long after my mother grew irritated with Diane to realize she'd been born again. Mom's annoyance grew to defensiveness when Diane started trying to save us kids. It turned to outright belligerence when Diane had the audacity to try to save my mother. No matter how heated their conversations, Diane always ended them with an invitation for my mother to attend a Sunday or Wednesday service. Yes, she had joined her mother's church.

"You would be embraced by everyone," Diane assured Mom.

My mother didn't believe her. "They would treat me like one of them?"

"Well," Diane halted, then said what was on her mind, "With all that makeup you wear, they'd know you aren't yet saved."

Only one perspective offended my mother worse than rebuking her soul—insulting her sense of style. Though not a natural beauty, my mother was always attractive, and worked hard to remain so. Without fail, she got her hair styled every week. She was the first woman among all friends and relatives to get fake fingernails glued over her own so she could clean house as vigorously as she loved and still have perfectly polished nails when she and Dad socialized on weekends. She never just dressed, even to run errands. She coordinated outfits. Earrings, shoes, rings, purse, they all accentuated, and matched the precise hue of her ensemble. Naturally, she was as meticulous about her lipstick shade, the breadth and sweep of her rouge, the richness of her eyeshadow and pencil-tip perfection of her eyeliner. Suggesting she wore too much makeup was tantamount to questioning the colors priests wore during various holy seasons.

Not only would my mother not set foot in Aunt Diane's church after that comment, but she wouldn't even talk to her about religion or God. The mere mention of the name "Jesus," with its charismatic, fundamentalist overtones, made her cringe.

Besides talking only about God, Diane changed her everyday life. She refused to go to the cinema, no matter what the movie. She said she went once after being born again, and she "knew" that Jesus didn't go into that dark movie house with her. So she never went again. The accident, and her transformation occurred after she told me I didn't have to offer to play "Do It Again" every time she visited. Ironically, given its title, I knew for certain never to ask the new Aunt Diane if she wanted to hear the song with me. Listening to contemporary music, and many other activities that felt so routine I didn't even question, Aunt Diane was determined never to do again.

Her faith gave her a new assertiveness. Whereas she used to be a good listener without opinions that stirred controversy into any conversation, now she had a keyhole eye on one topic—saving the rest of us from the lulling damnation of Catholicism. She not only talked about her church, but she kept inviting us to join her at a service. Barely 13 at the time, I considered going. Truthfully, I wasn't curious about her church service. But, despite how she had changed, I still liked Aunt Diane.

One characteristic my sister Judy and I both share is feeling compassion for the ostracized. Throughout elementary school, we both befriended classmates that nobody else liked. After one of her nerdy classmate's mother died, Judy rode bikes with this girl with a crooked mouth that made her slur her words. As far back as first grade, I invited a quiet boy with black metal-framed glasses and an irregular shaped head to my seventh birthday party. What I remember most about that party was overhearing his mother thank mine for letting me invite her son. So far, no one in school had ever invited him to anything. My birthday is in May, so he had been ignored all of first grade.

The more other relatives resisted "holy roller Diane," as she became known, the nicer I wanted to be to her. I could never tell if Uncle Stan was put off by Diane's newfound reason for living. He was always inattentive to her. If he was ignoring her now because she had Jesus, I distinguished no difference in their interactions.

Every time Diane asked my parents if she could bring any of us kids to church with her, my dad politely declined. My mother didn't even respond. Diane then started inviting us to church events. Nothing even piqued their interest until she asked my dad if she could bring us to a showing of the movie *The Cross and the Switchblade*. The title meant nothing to him, but when she said it starred Pat Boone, Dad seemed to ease his resistance. He liked Pat Boone and many similar singers from the 1950s. Mom's taste in music evolved past that traditional style years earlier. At night while she ironed, my mother listened to Herb Alpert & the Tijuana Brass, Tom Jones, or Barry White. When Dad did home repairs, he listened to Ferrante & Teicher and Mario Lanza.

Dad knew what we could expect from a Pat Boone movie. He'd seen *April Love* and *State Fair*. Although he never discouraged us from liking what was currently popular, he had a soft spot for wholesome nostalgia. What harm could a Pat Boone movie possibly do?

Ray and I went with Aunt Diane to her church to watch the movie. They showed it in their "Fellowship Hall"—which was a lot like the big "Activity Room" at St. Linus School where we had summer garage sales and the fourth graders' annual Christmas play. I don't remember much about the movie, except that it made a greater impression on Ray than on me.

Once we'd gone to Aunt Diane's church and hadn't lost our souls or renounced Catholicism, my parents relaxed their resistance to Aunt Diane's persistent requests for us kids to join her at a service. I don't know what changed, but one Friday evening my sister Judy agreed to go to a special revival service Aunt Diane seemed particularly excited about. Having spent most of my childhood learning about life from watching shows and afternoon movies on television, the only revival I'd ever seen was in *Elmer Gantry*. I was so naïve I thought Fire and Brimstone preaching meant that the service would end by literally setting the building on fire, as had occurred while Jean Simmons preached away sin as the flame-engulfed revival tent crumbled to ashes around her. Though a little scared, it sure made me curious. Once my parents said Judy could go, I wanted to, also.

As I entered Aunt Diane's church, I was stunned by its stark white blandness. Growing up Catholic, our church was cluttered with ornamentation: wooden carvings of The Stations of the Cross around the walls, light glistening through colorful stained-glass windows, a crucifix, and statues of Jesus and Mary and saints holding up one hand in a gesture of benediction. During a mass, there were always plenty of visual distractions to look at when the priest droned on too long. Here, they only had empty walls and a huge, rustic cross at the altar. Jesus wasn't even on it.

The minister was an older lady. As I expected, she wore no makeup, like Aunt Diane. I was not surprised she didn't wear a colorful robe, like our priests. I expected her to have a soft, flowing white dress like Jean Simmons billowing around the revival tent in *Elmer Gantry*. Instead, this stocky woman with a cropped hairdo and masculine chin wore a heavy cream-colored evening gown. It had a suggestion of embroidery and formed a straight, unmoving hem at her clunky shoes that clopped whenever she stepped off the carpeted chancel and onto the wooden floor where rows of benches were sprinkled with people.

At St. Linus' Friday mass before first period, the front pews were packed with us elementary students and our teachers, and a few old people scattered behind us. On Sunday, multigenerational families filled the sanctuary pews with people, male and female, of all ages and heights. But there weren't that many people in Aunt Diane's vanilla church. Those in attendance were older females. If it weren't for a spattering of people who didn't fit the demographic, I could have easily been sitting in a church filled with members of Baka's pinochle group.

Aunt Diane introduced us to Sister Gert, the minister. With that title, I thought Diane meant that the minister was a nun. But in reply, Sister Gert greeted Sister Diane and welcomed me, Brother Roger, to Jesus' house.

The service started with music, lots of music. At St. Linus, we sang, but stood firmly in place, and never touched each other during songs such as "Priestly People" or "By Our Love." When the music rattled the rafters here, people fidgeted and clapped and whooped like extras behind Olivia de Havilland in *The Snake Pit*. Even Mrs. Martinez next to me trembled like Elvis before she started clapping to the beat.

When she saw me locked stiff on immovable legs, gripping the seatback in front of me, she leaned over so I could hear her over the piano and tambourines. "Join in. You're clapping for Jesus."

I looked at my sister, on the other side of Aunt Diane. She wasn't moving either.

As the rumbling piano tones faded, I watched Sister Gert move into the aisle. I expected her to start a speech. Instead, she closed her eyes and summoned Jesus to enter the room.

I looked around, wondering if His spirit would waft in. People stood, mumbling or rocking or inert with closed-eye intensity. Something was about to happen. I remembered an illustration in a catechism book with licks of red flame above the head of each apostle awaiting Jesus in the Upper Room. I glanced toward people's heads, waiting for them to ignite like a pilot light. It was when I looked behind me I saw one of the few men in the sanctuary. He and a woman sat with no one else near them. She was fair and pretty. He had an unseasonably beautiful tan and golden, wavy hair. He was about the most handsome man I'd ever seen. He didn't see me, but I watched him long enough to tell he was only here to please the woman sitting beside him. When she quaked with the same anticipatory posture as most everyone else in the room, he sat immobile. He didn't appear confused and nervous like me, but curious, and certainly not swept into the flurry of salvation apparently swirling unseen through most of these believers.

Then somebody from the far corner of the church called out in a foreign language. The next moment, someone starting hollering in English. At first, I thought the second person was yelling at the first person to stop interrupting what was happening. Then I realized they *were* what everyone was waiting for. Their bilingual exchange stopped, Sister Gert raised her thick arms high into the air in praise, and then beseeched Spirit to come again and say more. It occurred to me that the foreigner was doing what Aunt Diane had described as speaking in tongues.

What am I doing here?

I'd never been in a room so primed to detonate. To that date, I'd only taken one plane ride, but the similarity was unmistakable. The anticipation felt like cabin pressure.

Beside me, Aunt Diane, her arms straight up like Gert's, burst into a jackhammering vocal tirade. Her small spout of a mouth rolled R's and flittered her tongue with a barrage of indistinguishable words. She sounded like a Middle Eastern auctioneer.

From the other side of the room, someone else ranted in English through booming, angry tones. The meter of their overlapping monologues made something obvious: the hollerer across the room was interpreting Diane's words.

She had described this phenomenon before, but I didn't know what she meant by the Spirit entering her to reveal a message in God's language and needing an interpreter. I couldn't make out the words yelled in English. To my left, Aunt Diane was rattling and quivering from Spirit, and Mrs. Martinez at my right leaned into me and assured, "That's Jesus. He's come to save you." She actually smiled. "He's here for you."

When the tongue-flapping ended, and the symphony of *Amens* and ecstatic *Halleluiahs* faded to whispers, Sister Gert planted her trunk-like legs so wide the material of her dress pulled taut. Her arms now spread out instead of up, she offered a guttural invitation for anyone not yet saved to come to the chancel and turn his life over to Jesus.

So far as I could tell, she was talking to my sister, me, and the handsome guy behind us. We were the only three in the church that night who looked as though we didn't belong.

I glanced toward my sister. She was five years older than I, and much more adventurous. She didn't move, but not out of fear or belligerence. Like me, I think she was taken aback. Neither of us knew what to do. I looked at Aunt Diane.

"It's okay," she said in the sweetest tone. "It's time."

I didn't make the decision to go toward Sister Gert. Mrs. Martinez took my arm. Because she moved like a mole and her limbs hung like willow branches, I never suspected her to have the vigor to manhandle me to the altar. I was too stunned to protest. Diane followed. I glanced behind me. Judy advanced with us until we reached Sister Gert.

"On your knees," Sister Gert instructed.

I looked at Diane for reassurance. She nodded.

"You, too," Gert told Judy.

I don't remember seeing anything for the next several minutes. Once we knelt, our little circle was shrink-wrapped by several of the faithful who came forward to pray over us and lay hands on us.

I was unaccustomed to being touched so much. My family had never been very physically intimate. Baka didn't hug. Whenever we grandkids kissed her goodbye, she extended a cheek. Grandma Leslie would have been the most likely to hold us, but crippling arthritis in her back and neck made squeezing painful.

Grandma was a single parent. Without strong male role models to follow, my dad developed very strict and lofty ideas about being a man. He developed most of those concepts through radio programs like *The Lone Ranger*, whose heroism intensified by being distant.

Like Baka, my mother needed plenty of social distance around her to be comfortable. Although I loved and needed my mother voraciously as a child, I don't have memories of her holding me. The most affectionate proof I have of my mother's physical affection appears in an old slide of me as a toddler curled up asleep on her lap. We are on a bus. Her right arm is not resting on my back but is extended over the seatback. Her right hand is under her chin. She is not looking at me or the camera but staring out the bus window.

As if a coven of female hands clawing at my shoulders wasn't disconcerting enough, Sister Gert pressed her palm against the crown of my head the way bullies hold their victim's head underwater. If I weren't so confused by the rash of unfamiliar sensations, I might have been scared. I couldn't lift my head to see how Judy was responding to any of this.

One of the women—her voice didn't sound like Mrs. Martinez, and I knew it wasn't Aunt Diane—instructed me, "Ask Jesus into your heart."

When I didn't say anything, she must have understood that I didn't know how.

"Say, 'Come to me, Jesus.'"

"Come to me, Jesus," I repeated with her same demanding inflection.

Nothing new happened—just the paws and the palms and the murmurings of the female congregation praying over me.

"Again," that lady told me. "Keep saying it until you feel Jesus enter your heart." Then she modeled once more, "'Come to me, Jesus. Come into my heart.'"

I repeated what she said, but never too loudly. While begging for Jesus, I was most concerned about not wanting to seem foolish to the gorgeous man who didn't come to the altar to get saved, too.

With the auditory dust of women's prayers hovering over Judy and me, I continued to follow the woman's instructions. "Come to me, Jesus," I asked. When the woman leaned in more fervently with her instructions to keep repeating the plea, I echoed with more zeal, "Come to me, Jesus. Come into my heart."

The canopy of females remained over Judy and me. The decibel of their cries increased, so I asked louder and louder, "Come to me, Jesus! Come to me!"

I felt swept into the excitement. I had never experienced anything quite like this laying of hands and "halleluiah" praying. My senses were overwhelmed. I didn't hear my sister begging Jesus to save her. Even if I opened my eyes, I was so confined in the circle of women that I couldn't have turned to see what impression my spiritual pleas had on the bronzed handsome man.

The women's fervor abated before mine did. As I kept chanting, "Come to me, Jesus, save me," the woman beside me changed her instructions. "He came to you, son. You're saved. Now thank Him."

I hadn't felt any shift. Nothing new brightened my heart. As mechanically as I had obeyed the first directive, I changed to the second. "Thank You, Jesus. Thank You, Jesus. Thank You, Jesus."

Several of the women above me were thanking Jesus, too. I did as I was told. I came to the altar, begged as they suggested, and didn't run when so many pawed at me. But I sensed no difference in my heart thanking Jesus than I did begging for His arrival.

I didn't know what to expect, but I wasn't lighter or wiser or happier. I didn't feel any more kinship with these strangers as they softened their grasp of my shoulders and eased off my back and head. Despite every "glory" and "see the wonders of God!" that followed, I felt the same. I didn't blame Jesus for not coming to me. I just figured I must have done it wrong.

When we were helped to our feet, I could tell that Judy had not found Jesus either. I knew this expression. She was pissed. I discovered later she felt betrayed by Aunt Diane for tricking us into attending a service where, Judy recognized more clearly than I, Diane (and maybe her mother) had brought us with the intention of saving our souls.

Although we knew it didn't work on us, Aunt Diane seemed to believe otherwise. She floated back to our pew triumphant as Angel Gabriel. She had been a good steward of God. If we didn't find Jesus that night, it wasn't because she had not done her part. While standing between us, she had spoken in tongues and summoned the Holy Spirit in our midst. Then she and Mrs. Martinez brought us under the blessed hand of Sister Gert and the faithful of the church, opening our souls to beckon Jesus. I never had the heart to tell Aunt Diane that Jesus was a no-show.

Diane didn't remain our aunt much longer. A few years as Uncle Stan's dismissed wife and her could-have-been-fatal car crash led her to find something more. It made sense that what she rejected about her mom—the Holy rolling through life toward the pearly gates—became the very avenue she took once the car crash made critical the need for something meaningful.

Throughout my childhood, I had many devout relatives fulfilled in their Catholic faith. One of my mother's cousins was a priest. Some favorite aunts and great aunts attended mass daily and went to sleep every night saying the rosary. What they believed, they apparently always believed, and it fed their souls for a lifetime.

Diane's circumstance was different. She started Catholic, at least in name and by infant baptism thanks to her father, but she found Jesus in response to unhappiness and a jarring accident. Although her life became more singularly purposeful, I think she traded in what remained of her happiness for an assurance that she'd eventually reclaim it eternally in Heaven. Every simple joy-filled moment I recall of Aunt Diane occurred before her accident. I was most stirred by the simplicity of my favorite image of Diane. At gentle sunset, her face glowing like a fresco, she nestled into the weave of an inexpensive lawn chair on her unfinished patio, after-work beer in hand, her little spout of a mouth stretched by an escapist smile as she watched her dog Lovey playing in their backyard.

Though it robbed her of this natural joy that made her angelic, I admired her for finding a cause. Emerging unscratched from that crushed heap of metal that once was a mail truck, she had a profound awakening. It torched her marital disappointment and caregiver exhaustion and sent her searching. She didn't search far. She'd been dropping her mother off at that church since her father died.

When I considered what I could learn from the conversion that didn't work, I wondered if maybe what we're looking for is always right before us. Perhaps what we want or think we need is not some deep, lost, or hidden Holy Grail only found at the end of a heroic quest. Aunt Diane's journey suggested that maybe enlightenment—our joy, our reason for celebrating our soul—is something already in our lives we finally just notice. I didn't feel the joy of Jesus while being pawed by a pup tent of hovering hands and intimidating voices pounding instructions at me and imploring penetration from spirit. But I did feel stirred to attraction and intrigue by the presence of a gorgeous blond man who seemed as equally out of place in that setting as I. Seeing him stirred my physical passion and emotional hunger. I guess, in the end, Jesus was there after all. He was sitting in the back of the sanctuary, a misfit like me, suggesting hope that I squelched because, at the time, he represented what I really wanted and could not allow myself to accept.

But that angel of masculine beauty awakened me to a struggle I was too terrified to acknowledge, but my heart would not ignore. Aunt Diane's journey suggested that what I wanted I already had and only needed to awaken to. I began a spiritual quest. Too ashamed to come to terms overtly with the truth of who I was, I took the first steps deeper within, hoping I could find answers, and peace, in secret.

12

I'm Filthy

I didn't feel the same kind of acceptance from my other relatives as I did from Aunt Diane. I was different, and it scared me. In the middle-America, Polish-Catholic bubble that was my world as a child, I recognized very little diversity, and certainly no acceptance of it.

As I imagine most families would be, mine was especially proud of its heritage. One great aunt affixed a bumper sticker onto the glass of her living room curio that trumpeted, "I'm Polish from the top of my head to the tips of my toes." Dangling from the side of that curio was an oversized rosary. Hanging beside that curio was a 1963 calendar with a portrait of John F. Kennedy, our Catholic President. When my immediate family moved to Texas in 1976, my great aunt still had that Kennedy calendar on her wall. Such pride clarified and reinforced with great strength and cohesion who we were as an extended family. When I knew myself only as a Polish Catholic boy, that defining clarity comforted. Once I acknowledged that I was also gay, it strangled my hope of being able to remain myself without becoming a family outcast.

Perhaps out of fear I noticed, on both sides of my family, the potential for being ostracized. Uncle Stan's sister, and my mother's half-sister, Beverly became a drug addict after she married at age 18. Thereafter, both she and her husband were in and out jail often. When freed, she lived with her mom, my Baka. During those years we saw a lot of Aunt Bev. We younger kids thought she was hilarious. Unaware that she was usually high, we thought she was just ditzy and accident-prone. Once Aunt Bev took us to the roller rink. Not paying attention, she exited through an emergency door that set off a blaring alarm. She took off running toward the car, and the rest of us scampered after her. Over our laughter, we could still hear the alarm down the block as she raced away before the police arrived.

Aunt Bev was as skinny as the guys who got sand kicked in their faces in comic book muscle-building ads. Yet she was freakishly strong. Since the 1950s, my parents owned a powerful Raymond Loewy Singer Vacuum cleaner with a sturdy metal handle. One day as she casually vacuumed our living room, the pipe cracked in half. Stunned, Bev stared at the pipe still in her grip while at her feet the motionless vacuum still whirred air into the bloated canvas bag.

Not all episodes under the influence were so benign. During nighttime highs on more dangerous drugs, Bev had episodes of crazed violence, of which Baka was often the victim. Afterward, most of the extended family shunned her. The rest would be coldly civil to her, at best. As a result, Bev usually skipped family events. At one funeral, I understood why. My mom and I sat with Bev at the wake because no one else would even approach her. I couldn't imagine how she could help from being hurt. But in her usual fun and self-deprecating way, she acknowledged her ostracism by joking, "What, do my feet stink or something?" Funny or not, Aunt Bev had lost her place in the family.

My father's relatives had an equally cookie-cutter version of how people should act, and what "kind" of people could marry into the family. Although no counter-culture rebel like my mom's half-sister, Dad's sister Dolly marched to the beat of her own drummer, who, it appeared was in an oompah band. In 1955, only 10 years after the war that many of her male relatives fought in, she married a German. For a while, her decision had catastrophic repercussions.

Over the decades, the family didn't relax their restrictive attitudes. Years later, one great aunt suggested—quite innocently as a curiosity, not a point of contention—that we might have some Czech in our bloodline. The family was outraged that she would even suggest such an abhorrent possibility.

I thought nothing of it. Our ancestors were from outside Krakow, not far from the Poland/Czech border. To me both Eastern European cultures seemed very similar.

"We are Polish!" My great uncle banged his fist on the table, stormed off, and refused to talk to that sister for days. The rest of the relatives in that conversation sided with him.

A comment from another of my dad's aunts cut more personally. At my grandmother's dining room table, my great aunt pointed out an article about a suspected gay celebrity in her *National Enquirer*. "I think that's filthy," she sneered. Her expression brought to mind the image of the disgust that contorted my mother's face during the lesbian wedding on Tom Snyder's late night talk show. The incongruity between believing I belonged to a very loving close-knit family, and their unfiltered disdain for difference convinced me that I was safer hiding than being honest about what I could no longer deny I was.

Nothing suggested to me that anyone else thought I might be gay. If I had suspected others were questioning my sexuality, I couldn't imagine how much more terrifying the prospect of coming to terms with myself would have seemed. Ironically, the dark place in which I was burying myself deeper and deeper felt vacuous and foreboding, yet in its secrecy, safe.

13

Dismissed

Though not shunned as a boy, I was accustomed to being ignored and dismissed by male relatives. So when my Uncle Tom agreed to be my confirmation sponsor in 1975, I felt proud. At the altar when I knelt to receive my blessing from Father Kinneally, Uncle Tom, as instructed, rested his hand on my shoulder. It felt approving. During what was supposed to be only a religious rite, I felt a sense of initiation into a brotherhood of my male relatives. It didn't last.

The following month, Uncle Tom visited the family. Instead of hanging out with Mom and the women, as I used to do before I felt more included and mature, I stayed with the men. With Dad and Randy and me, Uncle Tom shared how he had accepted a challenge to run a 10-minute mile. Like most of my male relatives of that era, he smoked and drank a lot. But he went into his version of training and cut back on cigarettes. Plus, he was at least ten years younger than my dad, so he had age on his side.

He told my dad about the psychology he would employ—determining what song he would sing in his head as he ran the laps during his challenge so he wouldn't be thinking about running or leg pains or shortness of breath. Dad agreed that distracting his mind with something rhythmic would help. Randy suggested he pick a single lane and stick with it, so that changing running lanes would not refocus his mind on what his body was doing.

"I think you can do it," I declared with the same enthusiasm that Dad and Randy responded to him.

He didn't reply. Neither did Dad or Randy. They continued sharing their strategies and psychologies as if I weren't there.

I thought perhaps they hadn't heard me. So I repeated, with a little more volume, "I think you can do it, Uncle Tom."

No response. So I inserted a question. "How much longer do you have to train before you take the laps?" It was a sound question, one that certainly contributed to the conversation, one that even Dad or Randy might have asked.

Uncle Tom continued his discussion with the two of them as if I weren't there. As I walked away unnoticed, I decided I had read too much into that affirming moment of initiation with his hand on my shoulder. At my confirmation, I felt as though I finally belonged. Now I not only felt isolated, but I also sensed a foolish embarrassment for feeling something warm and encouraging that wasn't shared. I no longer wanted to remain so close to the women in my life, so I'd pulled away. Like a pride of male lions, I thought I would automatically be accepted into their number. But I wasn't. I thought I had had my initiation moment when I selected Uncle Tom to be my confirmation sponsor. He had agreed and had stepped up to the altar with me to support who I was becoming.

Unequipped at that age to keep perspective, I generalized what that encounter with Uncle Tom meant. I concluded that if he could stand behind me at the altar to support me, and then dismiss me as he had before, then I must be alone about how I felt and what I perceived about situations. That hurt. In one sense, it mattered because it suggested that I was more of a social misfit than I had even thought before.

But something sadder and more frightening latched onto my mind with that insight. The rituals and initiations of my faith didn't *really* apply to me because I was gay. Uncle Tom had agreed to be my confirmation sponsor, then immediately went back to ignoring me as if I were still the odd little boy I suspected most men thought I was. In that same way, I believed God probably wanted nothing to do with me, either. It was one kind of isolation to feel alone among my peers, and then my family. It was more shattering to sense I was being ignored by God.

For a while, I hoped that somehow I misunderstood what being gay meant. After all, I was sheltered and naïve, and knew nothing about sex. When I was about ten, I asked my dad to explain it to me. We were in the kitchen, and Randy decided to stay to hear dad's explanation, and more likely, to see my reaction.

"In sexual intercourse," my dad got as stiff and flat as a cardboard cutout, "a man inserts his penis into a woman's vagina and ejaculates."

When we were little kids, my mom and Baka always shifted into Polish when discussing something juicy they didn't want us to know. Dad's answer didn't sound Polish, but except for "man" and "woman," I didn't recognize a single key word in that sentence.

"Oh," I nodded. I'm sure my dad could read on my face that I didn't understand a word he told me. But he made a quick exit, leaving Randy and me alone.

"Do you understand what he said?" Randy barely talked to me at all. I couldn't believe he was going to tell me this. But I was still curious, so I nodded my head no.

"A guy sticks his dick in a woman and comes."

While in that sentence I understood all the vocabulary except the last word, I still didn't grasp the mechanics of how that worked. "Oh," I nodded, same as I did with Dad. This time, I was the one who left the room.

Although it provided no enlightenment about sex, my inquiry gave me one obvious insight. I either needed to expand my vocabulary or accept the fact that I still had no idea what sex was, how the act worked, and why I had no desire to do to a woman whatever it is they said men do.

Once, when my cousin Lisa was visiting, she brought up the topic of sex. She was about nine and I was eleven, and we both came from families with four children. It became immediately clear that we were equally naïve. Our entire catalog of knowledge on the subject led us to agree, with crinkled noses and a little uncertain disgust, that our parents both did it four times. When we realized that our Aunt Greta and Uncle Steve had six children, we were wide-eyed with awe that anyone could do it that much!

Eager to learn more, I suggested to Lisa we look up information in the set of World Book Encyclopedias in my dad's basement office. We snuck down there, and I immediately pulled out the S volume to find "sex." *What if there's even a diagram!* I marveled as I flipped to those pages. Nothing.

Meantime, Lisa picked up the D volume.

"What are you looking up?"

"Dick."

We learned nothing that day.

I led a very safe and protected childhood, thanks to my diligent parents. It only struck me much later that, even when I developed curiosity about sex, the thought of experimenting with anyone never occurred to me. Instead, I again turned to movies and television to fulfill the increasing fantasies that teemed through my young mind.

As my sexual appetite surged in puberty, my fascination with handsome stars became the springboard for many a nighttime fantasy. Nothing sexual had to occur in a movie or television show to spark new imaginings. I could watch an old Montgomery Clift or Rock Hudson movie on the tiny black and white portable TV and for the next week create multiple stories where the actor and I became best friends who grew to love each other intimately. In their primes, when studios created idealized, heterosexual biographies of these stars, I saw nothing in my Hollywood magazines to indicate any actor was gay. How crushing that, with these two favorite stars in particular, I spent my youth enamored of them, and so wrongly assuming that they would find strange and off-putting everything I was thinking about them.

Most intriguing, although prompted by physiological urges, my fantasies were not sexual in nature. I didn't understand heterosexual sex, so I surely couldn't imagine what two men might do. But that wasn't what I ached for anyway. From men only, I wanted affection and intimacy. I wanted to feel noticed. My innocence freed me to create all sorts of wonderful fantasies that filled my lonely heart more than they ever satisfied a sexual urge. Because I consistently exercised my creative impulses at a pivotal stage of brain development, I feel certain these scenarios honed my desire and skill for creative writing. But at the loneliest nadir of my existence, they also left me feeling more disenfranchised. During that time, when I read the line "No man is an island," my first thought was, *John Donne must not have been gay.* (According to some literary analyses of his poems, I might have misunderstood Donne as much as I had Montgomery Clift and Rock Hudson.)

Ultimately, I concluded that no one in the world was like me. I thought I was completely alone in what I wanted. But the train had left the station. I knew what I wanted, even if I could never have it beyond imagining scenarios with handsome stars I would never meet. Once I decided that my emotional and sexual desires did not match anyone else, I laid tracks in any tunnel that could hide me and determined that I could never share with anyone what I thought or felt. That meant I was not only alone then, but the conclusion I had drawn suggested that I would be alone forever.

As my realization of being gay solidified, I felt betrayed by God. What had I done to be punished with desires that damned me for eternity? As awareness of what I felt and who I was became undeniable, I had determined that I would never act on these feelings. Long before my body developed arousal reflexes, the desire I felt was emotional. I hungered for closeness and understanding. Only years later did my want of compassion merge with passion. All these insights came as a result of forces growing from who I always was, with powers so natural and deep-seated there was never a time when I didn't feel them.

Instead of their constancy breeding comfort from familiarity, they loomed larger and more terrifying to me. Because they always had been part of me, I couldn't imagine my life ever changing for the better. So I just kept withdrawing further into myself, even as I saw it leading me into the darkness of my own soul.

Isolated

As my self-awareness clarified, I was so determined to hide my sexual identity I never considered that any of my other classmates might be struggling with the same self-concept. In third grade, my best friend was a boy named Johnny Cipriano. Because he lived just one block from us at the corner where I used to catch the public-school bus for kindergarten, Mom let me walk to his house to play. He was an only child with so many toys we sometimes found board games he hadn't even opened. Coming from a house with four kids, I couldn't imagine, but I was fascinated. I don't remember why Johnny and I became friends. But I remember vividly why we stopped.

When the weather warmed in the spring of that school year, the snow melted off the parking lot so we could run and play during recess. Some girls started teasing Johnny because he was a little effeminate. He responded by telling them he was in love with them. He puckered his lips so tightly he looked more like a fluted vase than Casanova and spent our outdoor time chasing those taunting girls around the parking lot to kiss them. He bounded toward them, stiff feet clomping in unbroken leather shoes, hands flexed against his hips like startled butterflies. The girls shrieked and outran him. While their expressions conveyed repulsion, their giddy cackles suggested something I couldn't understand: they seemed equally repulsed and amused by his advances.

His actions embarrassed me. Even puckered and chasing girls, he was the most effeminate boy I ever saw. When he went after one girl from our class infamous for picking her freckled nose and eating what she dug out, I ended my connection with Johnny that moment. I don't remember a confrontation or even conversation. I only knew that before we walked back into the school to finish our afternoon classes, I was done being his friend.

After that event, I lost and gained other friendships. In middle school grades, I had a good friend named Linus Erlingis. (His musical name alone made his friendship worth exploring.) He was rather shy. When we rode our bikes through the neighborhood, we never had much to say. One field trip, our class went to see the movie *Sounder*. Going to a Catholic school, we didn't have buses, so parent volunteers had to drive. Linus' mother took a carload of boys that included Linus and me. I ended up in the front seat between Mrs. Erlingis and another adult chaperone.

Until I reached high school I was seldom overcome by dark sadness. For some reason I felt shy and alone on the way to the movie. While Linus and the other boys talked and laughed, I sat silently watching the road ahead. Mrs. Erlingis, who spoke like Irene Dunne in *I Remember Mama*, commented in the kindest intonation, "You're so quiet. You seem like a sad little boy."

"I'm okay," I lied.

That brief interaction made an impact. First, it taught me something I didn't know about myself. Her compassionate comment was heartwarming. I felt affirmed by the fact that a stranger—and an adult—noticed how I was feeling and cared enough to comment about it. I also felt guilty for not being happy because, as I had heard throughout my childhood, God had given me so much to be grateful for. Like many of my personal life experiences, it was further shaped by a movie I saw. While feeling guilty for not appreciating how much God had given me in my life, I watched the movie *Sounder* about a loving family in a society that treated them with injustice and cruel disdain. When the character David Lee, who was about my age when I saw the movie, took the cake his mother baked so beautifully to his father in prison, and the officer jabbed and mangled it searching for a hidden weapon, I heard Mrs. Erlingis gasp.

She showed such compassion for a family very different from what I knew as a boy. I grew up in a White, middle-class suburb of Detroit. I didn't know and had little grasp of how even to understand the troubles faced by a Black sharecropper family in the South during The Great Depression.

That day opened so many worlds to me. Mrs. Erlingis had a heart like no one else I knew. On our way home, I couldn't even find words to thank her for noticing me, and speaking to me. I can't say that that single comment during that ride changed the direction of my life, but the timing of it resonated so powerfully it remains one of the most emotionally impactful tiny moments from my childhood.

Throughout most of my years at St. Linus, I had many friends. I felt comfortable around smart, studious, and polite boys like John Machniak, who wore a trademark red vest to school, and Jeff Gwinn, who sold me his copy of an old MAD Magazine issue I really wanted.

The closest friend I shut out before I finished school at St. Linus was my good buddy, Steve Hideg. Throughout our last years at St. Linus, we hung out together, walking around during recess. We had little in common, really. He liked science. I liked the arts. A die-hard Trekkie, he was appalled when I told him I never watched *Star Trek*, but I liked *Lost in Space*.

"Science fiction fans think *Lost is Space* is crap," he told me. I didn't care. Wanting to be loyal to anyone connected to *The Poseidon Adventure*, I became of fan of *Lost in Space* because it was created by producer Irwin Allen. Steve offer sound arguments why I should also hate *Lost in Space*—the fake foam rocks, the inane Reynold's Wrap aliens, Penny Robinson's "blooping" pet chimpanzee. For me, loyalty trumped logic. I supported Irwin Allen by being a fan of *Lost in Space*, and I never developed an interest in *Star Trek*.

We didn't have a band at St. Linus, but Steve was a good musician and followed local musical productions. I had memorized all the dialog to *The Poseidon Adventure*, and he knew the entire book of *Guys and Dolls* from a current production at the nearest Catholic high school, Divine Child. Some days we spent our entire recess creating conversations from snippets of dialog from each. Because we loved an intellectual challenge, those afternoons were among the most fun and funny we ever shared. Ironically, during those times when we conversed for almost an hour saying absolutely nothing about ourselves, I felt closest to him.

After I realized how astute he was, I feared he would figure out what I had confirmed to my own terror and disgust. Steve pulled no punches. If he didn't like something or somebody, he told them. When asked a question by a teacher or authority figure, he answered with bold confidence. Once, a guest priest preparing our class for confirmation asked if any of us had ever considered becoming a priest or nun. Steve was the only one to raise his hand.

Shocked glares and snickers swarmed him like ants on picnic meat. His eyes grew the size of cherry tomatoes. "I didn't say I was going to do it," he announced to our peers. "He just asked if we ever thought about it." Steve returned every quizzical gaze with such authority, students withered. "Yeah. I thought about it . . . once."

I could imagine Steve being a physicist by day and playing trumpet at local clubs on weekends—a kind of Woody Allen Einstein. But in my mind, he was no priest.

Steve was heady and sometimes sarcastic. One Friday, Sr. Lidwina asked our class to remind her to take up next week's assignment on Tuesday instead of Wednesday. Steve immediately raised his hand.

"Yes?"

"Be sure to take up next week's assignment on Tuesday instead of Wednesday." He smiled at his own joke.

Sr. Lidwina's spine stiffened. She raised a crooked, aging finger. "You are an impertinent young man, Steve."

He reserved future snide attempts at humor for a less sophisticated audience of his peers.

I was not one of them. I didn't find his sarcasm funny, so he quit shooting barbs about other people to me because I wouldn't laugh at what I didn't think was funny.

Similarly, he also made clear that he found intolerable certain behaviors of mine. Once, he and I rode our bikes to my Baka's house. She let us sit in the breezeway and listen to albums on her stereo. She had Barbra Streisand's *Live Concert at the Forum* album.

As the record played, I studied the black and white album cover, holding it closer and closer to my face until the sketch of a somber Streisand revealed an abstract Morse Code of tiny dots and dashes. Absently, I sang along.

"Stop it."

I didn't even realize I had started. After a few more bars, I started again without thinking.

He stood. "Sing one more word and I'm going home."

At the time, I didn't realize I can't carry a tune. I also never considered that, because Steve had musical talent, he might have thought I was deliberately ruining the song. I wasn't. I got swept into music that moved me and was drawn to joining in. Although I had no context for it at the time, singing along to a Barbra Streisand song was probably the gayest behavior I ever showed in front of Steve. I had no idea that was the case. I liked what I liked and expressed appreciation for music by singing what I heard. In that moment, it never occurred to me that he might have demanded I stop because he saw, or even sensed, something so gay about it. I wasn't impersonating her or choreographing the song as I accompanied her. I just sat in Baka's worn out green upholstered chair looking at the faded album cover and singing. But it irked Steve to the point of giving me an ultimatum. If I planned to spend another second with him, I'd stop what I was doing. I added singing as one more natural inclination that I should never let others know I liked.

During our friendship, I don't think Steve ever suspected I was gay. But the thought of anyone figuring out what I knew terrified me. In response, one Saturday before we graduated from St. Linus when Steve was coming over to spend the day, I decided I could no longer be his friend without risking his figuring me out. He was bright. When he talked to people, he looked right into them and often spoke his observations about them with clinical accuracy.

As he biked to my house that morning, I was sitting on the front porch. He initiated conversation. I replied with clipped, one-word answers.

"What's the matter with you?"

"Nothing," I shrugged.

He tried starting a conversation on another topic. I remained aloof. My answers shrunk to curt, monosyllabic responses. Even I felt the chill of my dismissive insolence.

Although I was clearly acting out of character, Steve didn't persist in asking what was wrong. Instead, he mounted his bike again and said, "I don't have to put up with this." Without a "goodbye" he rode away. That marked the end of our friendship.

Systematically I disconnected from peers who cared about me and treated me well. In my attempt to hide the truth of which I was ashamed, I receded into an emotional space as small and dark as a confessional. I didn't trust that anyone on the other side of that stapled black veil would help hide my identity if the trap door slid open. Lonely and afraid, I was determined never to reveal my true feelings to anyone.

Friendless

Everything was about to change when I left St. Linus and started high school. That thought dragged me down with the weight of cement shoes. Since I was six years old, I had attended one grade school with the same students, familiar teachers, and an environment I knew. Loss of that familiarity terrified me.

Obsessing over my fear of change felt like taking short breaths as water filled my lungs. Hating who I was, and fearing anyone else would figure it out, I severed every human lifeline I had outside my immediate family. I survived with a love of movies and television, but I wasn't living. I felt empty and alone and missed every air bubble of potential hope drifting past me.

The traditional, huge-treat event for St. Linus' graduating eighth graders was a trip to Sandusky, Ohio for a day at Cedar Point amusement park. I went on the trip and spent the day alone. In part, I was hiding. But I knew even then, I also spent the day indulging my self-pity for having no friends. It became my identity. I saw how foolish that choice was. Even an old *I Love Lucy* episode reinforced the idiocy of my choice. Lucy feels betrayed by her friends and roams a park with a sign identifying her as "a friend of the friendless." It was silly and slapstick and rather stupid—all adjectives that could have awakened my soul to the absurdity of my choice to insulate my life for emotional safety, but instead discovering suffocation.

To further feed the inanity of my self-pity that day at Cedar Point, I decided I would go on a quest to purchase a souvenir for every one of my family members. That way I could not only feel lonely, but I could feel worse by doing something loving for others while I felt dismissed and forgotten. It didn't escape me, even in my underdeveloped 14-year-old brain, that I disengaged from my classmates to create a scenario in which I was the forgotten one. But if I were to hide or run from who I was and could not face, my convoluted logic told me that feeling sorry for myself was the only form of self-love I deserved. That it only made me feel worse was fitting. Self-pity didn't accelerate my downward spiral toward the pits of Hell—it placed me there instantly.

Still in the morning hours at Cedar Point, while selecting for my sister a souvenir vinyl pencil case shaped like a huge pencil with a zippered opening at the eraser (*how clever was that*, I thought, *a pencil-shaped pencil case!*) I ran into a group of four classmates.

"Are you by yourself?" one compassionate girl asked.

"I'm okay," I said. It felt very affirming to note that someone else had joined me in feeling sorry for poor, lonely Roger. Then I added vinegar to the sympathy wound. "I'm buying presents for my family."

"Do you want to spend the day with us?"

This was my chance to enjoy my day. A simple "Yes" would have let me feel included, maybe even embraced, in the familiarity of being accepted, as I always had been, as one of St. Linus' class of '75. "No, thank you," I replied with full metal jacket stupidity. "I'm okay alone."

They shrugged and walked away. Throughout the day I saw other classmates from a distance on that field trip. To boost my pity quotient, I walked the other way. My classmates' laughter and fatigue on the long bus ride home confirmed this Cedar Point outing as an eighth grade high point for most of their year. For me, it served only to convey what self-destructive social choices I was making, and how they trapped me in a whirlpool I didn't know how to escape.

In the rented bus on our ride home that evening, I enjoyed a conversation with Mary Pat Brogan. An earlier interaction with her illuminated a strength in me I didn't otherwise recognize. One preparation for our Holy Confirmation was to select a confirmation name. Yes, although legally our names remained what our parents gave us at birth, in the eyes of the Catholic Church, our new name, between our middle and last name, identified our new, theoretically self-committed Catholicism.

I chose as my confirmation name Thomas in honor of my confirmation sponsor, Uncle Tom. In May of 1975, I became Roger James Thomas Leslie. When the priests asked me which Saint Thomas I was naming myself after, I had to find a book of saints in the school library to discover what St. Thomases even existed. My primary choices were St. Thomas Aquinas, who embodied faith and reason, and St. Thomas More, a statesman and Renaissance humanist. In a decision exemplary of how my brain worked, I chose St. Thomas More because he was the subject of *A Man for All*

Seasons, a movie that won Best Picture, and Best Actor for Paul Scofield, at the 1966 Academy Awards.

Mary Pat was a feminist, in part, I suspect, as a reaction against the unwanted attention she received from boys because she physically developed so early, so much, and so perfectly. But Mary Pat was about intellect and social breakthroughs, and so she toyed with the idea of taking a male name, Michael, as her confirmation name. Her mother would have none of it.

Even in this context, my pop culture sensibilities proved a guiding force for social change. "There are women named Michael," I told Mary Pat while the two of us worked on a Friday art project together. "Michael Learned plays the mother on *The Waltons*."

Mary Pat's face brightened.

As proof I had no idea the rest of the world didn't put as much stock in entertainment trophies, I clinched my argument by adding, "She won the Best Lead Actress in a Drama Series Emmy the last *two* years!"

I don't know if Mary Pat even heard of the Emmys or if any of my arguments worked into convincing her mother that she could indeed choose a male confirmation name. But when we were confirmed, Michael she was.

On the late-night ride home from Cedar Point, Mary Pat and I were among the few students in our section of the bus who stayed awake. As she and I talked, I noticed that Mary Pat was not listening to me, but smiling wistfully at whatever she stared at in the seat in front of her. I looked at what had captivated her attention. Matt Biek, a tall dark-haired boy with a long neck and aspirations to play professional baseball, lay sleeping across the seat, his right knee bent so his legs formed a triangle, and his fingers tucked under the opposite arms.

Mary Pat looked at him starry-eyed the way actors do in movies when romantic violin strains begin. She smiled and said aloud, "He looks so innocent sleeping like that." She must have thought his crossed arms indicated he was cold, because she took off her jacket and covered him with it.

Mary Pat and Matt were not an item. At age 14, none of the eighth graders at St. Linus pursued romantic gestures any more than Dave Kosinski's friendship earrings to Mary Serwatowski. But for the first time in the flesh, not on screen, I saw, and felt because she was sitting beside me, the emanating warmth of physical attraction. As green as I was about infatuation even at that age, I could tell she liked him in this posture—sleeping and inaccessible—and not with a childhood crush that required some validation from Matt to feel complete.

Mary Pat was bold to share so unashamedly what she was feeling. To me she was very brave. I looked at Matt. Personally, I wasn't attracted to him, or any boys my age. But I recognized the innocence she described and realized that there were as many reasons to be attracted to someone as there were someones to be attracted to.

Until that interaction with Mary Pat, I reserved most of my physical attraction to adult actors in movies and on TV. But her courage inspired me to at least recognize and acknowledge, only to myself at this stage in life, when I was attracted to a guy I saw in person. In Mary Pat's twinkling gaze, and the sweet gesture of covering Matt because she thought he was cold, I connected sexual attraction with emotional tenderness. That union of flesh and heart solidified. From then on, even my sexual fantasies required a context of connecting emotionally. I have no way of knowing what prompts and perpetuates other guys' wet dreams, but even my fantasies left me thinking I was not like most other people. While physical attraction might inspire a fantasy, I felt sexually charged by affection and connection rather than body parts and Karma Sutra positions.

I guess I desired what I didn't have and wanted most. For me, especially in those dark ages that would continue in high school, fantasy temporarily freed me from the bonds of isolation I couldn't even find the surface to tread through. Unfortunately, it often left me too weak to even navigate through the simplest of social interactions.

16

Falling, Not Dancing

I did something cruel at the first dance I ever attended. Following our eighth-grade graduation ceremony, we ended our time at St. Linus at a farewell dance in the school activity room.

The nuns served punch and finger sandwiches at the louver doors that had served as our stage curtain for the 4th grade "Christmas around the World" play with Mary Serwatowski starring as Mrs. Claus. In that production I was Carl. With my sister Greta I explained yuletide traditions in Sweden. At the eighth-grade dance, I felt as if I were once again from the other side of the world. On one hand, I was lost and sad about a stage of my life officially ending that night. But more profoundly, in this very traditional boy-belongs-with-girl rite of passage, I saw myself as the only graduate not heading to a new phase that held promise of connection and love and success. My sense of loss was compounded by the fact that I could not pursue the same emotional and physical connections I assumed all my peers were taking for granted.

By dusk, the snacking was over, the lights were turned down, and the spinning glass prism overhead hypnotized the room with an invitation to dance. I don't know who created the playlist—probably one of the smart, outgoing students like Susan Kramer or Monique Zonca—but the music set a tone of warmth to ease our last-remnants-of-middle-school awkwardness. While eating and mingling, all the girls had stood in large clusters along one wall. In front of the opposite wall, the boys were either bunched in groups like Jets and Sharks or scattered in sparse pairs. I leaned against a stack of chairs and would probably have remained unnoticed except for my loud plaid jacket—white and brown and green—and shiny white and brown Winthrop oxfords.

With the music up and the lights down, both sexes started eyeing the group along the opposite wall. I never planned to dance that night. Except for wedding polkas, I didn't know how. More significantly, I didn't want to dance with a girl, and the idea of dancing with another boy was so foreign to the culture in which I was raised, I never even imagined such an idea. I just figured I would observe awhile then go home, leaving grade school forever behind me.

"Students," one of the nuns stepped to the center of the room after the first song that got only a few couples onto the dancefloor. "In order to get everybody dancing—"

Several students gasped. A lemon-sized lump in my throat kept me from even breathing.

Sister smiled. "Yes, *everybody*, we're going to have a dance where your partner has already been picked for you."

I had no idea where she was going with this.

"You're all going to share this next dance with your graduation partner."

For our graduation ceremony, boys processed into the church through one door, girls through an adjacent one. Each gender lined up alphabetically, which partnered me with Patti Kwatera. In classes when I sat behind her, she would often turn her large body around and whisper a snide observation about somebody that made me laugh.

Near the end of our grade school days, another female student whose last name came close to ours alphabetically enrolled in St. Linus. Stringy-haired Suzanne

Mulgrew made an indelibly bad impression as a slumber party guest when she blew her nose in the host's curtains. The next Monday at school, students were abuzz with disgusting details, and rife with new nicknames built around the word "snot." Rather than feeling mortified and apologizing, Suzanne liked negative attention. In scuffed white patent leather shoes she wore with no socks or hose, she clomped around school twisting her long fingers through a matted clump of brown hair and laughing to herself like a crazed indigent. It was hard to tell if she acted that way just to draw snickers and snarls, but she definitely basked in the curious stares. Even further, she languished in bullying others. Perhaps solely because my insecurity and confusion made me an easy target, I became her favorite bull's eye.

Once, when Patti made one of her caustic barbs about the new girl, Suzanne was close enough to hear. Instead of confronting Patti, who would have likely relished a battle of wits with her, Suzanne started a rumor that Patti and I were an item. Because Patti already had backbone, she wasn't a bit fazed by the lie. Socially immature and oversensitive, I was mortified. It had nothing to do with Patti being heavy. As hidden as I kept my interest in males, I resented anyone suggesting I had any such connection with a female.

The rumor was so obviously ludicrous no one bought it. Patti was obese and comically crabby, and I was a four-eyed, still underdeveloped teen who wore inexplicably oversized baggy pants and carried my copy of *The Poseidon Adventure* novel with me to every class. Still, Suzanne persisted because it clearly bothered me. With Suzanne seated so near us, I stopped laughing at Patti's snide asides. Eventually, she quit turning around. We didn't talk much the rest of the year. When we discovered we were partners at graduation practice, she rolled her eyes and I stiffened with discomfort.

Suzanne Mulgrew must have read my body language. "So romantic. You'll be walking down the church aisle together. Good practice for your wedding." Some of the students nearby laughed. Patti and I never said a word to each other at practice or at graduation.

When the announcing nun told us to find our graduation partner for the next dance, I darted to the boys' restroom and stayed there the duration of the song. I felt terrible. Suspecting that Patti thought she'd been abandoned because she was fat made me feel even worse. But I couldn't stand the triumphant grin slovenly Suzanne Mulgrew would surely enjoy watching me fumbling to hold Patti as she, I had no doubt, would have led our dance.

At the time, I was so self-absorbed, I only pictured Patti looking crushed when she realized that everybody was on the dancefloor except her, and I was nowhere to be found. Knowing Patti, it's even more likely that she made an indifferent exit from the activity room because she had as little interest in dancing with me. If I were directing a movie of that event, I would cut back and forth to shots of students dancing. Despite the awkwardness of immaturity, I would capture close-ups of their subtle smiles of feeling warm and included. In between, I would intersperse two sets of quick cuts. One would show me standing alone in the corner of the boys' bathroom, arms folded, never turning to face my reflection in the mirror beside me. Others were of Patti. Early in that snippet of a screenplay, I pictured her receding behind the nuns at the punch bowl, fighting back tears of rejection, a rotund version of Betsy Blair in *Marty*. But a later scenario had her shrugging with relief and making some caustic observation that made even the nuns laugh.

My movie fantasy, an emotional "safe space" to which I often escaped, ended with the last note of the partner dance song. Well into the next tune, I stepped out only as far as the hallway. Instead of turning left into the activity room, I took a few steps right to the accordion-fold metal gate that blocked the hall leading to the classrooms. Every day after school, tall gray custodian Gus secured that gate with a huge lock and chain. Peering through the diamond latticework, I realized I was looking at my past. I touched the chain that barred me from it. When this night ended, so would this stage of my life.

That gave me courage to go back into the activity room. If I wasn't in an emotional place to enjoy it, I could at least experience it until it ended. I looked around for Patti, mostly to make sure I stayed on the extreme other side of the room from her, but I never did find her. As I hid in the bathroom and then reflected sadly on the realization of irretrievable loss, she probably thought, *To hell with this*, and just went home. With Patti, that was entirely possible. At that stage in my life, I assumed everyone was more self-confident and socially developed than I. Her razorback demeanor and indifference-tinged humor confirmed with some certainty that Patti had found quite different ways than I to contend with growing pains.

In my hazy 14-year-old self-protectiveness, I didn't think any more about Patti the rest of that event. I stood at the edge of the dancefloor, not quite knowing what to do with my hands. Unexpectedly, sweet, compassionate Andrea Standish took pity on me. She tugged at my fidgeting fingers and led me to the dancefloor at the beginning of the final song of the night—Bread's "I Want to Make It with You." Noting how everyone else was dancing, I let Andrea pull me close to her. She encircled my neck with fleshy, heavy arms. I wrapped my arms around her thick waist. She was not the size of Patti, but she was a stocky, tall girl. Her body was surprisingly trunk-like in its sturdiness. When I danced polkas with female relatives, we interlocked arms, or wrapped them around each other's backs as we hop-step-stepped facing the same direction. But I had never held another person close and rocked in her arms. Although throughout the dance my lower back strained to keep me balanced against her girth, I felt warm and accepted.

Before I realized I was gay, I took for granted my sense of belonging with the classmates at St. Linus. In the arms of a girl, I rediscovered a sense of connectivity that was safe only if I kept secret the truth of who I was. Thanks to compassionate Andrea, I felt a brief reconnection with what I had severed. It provided fleeting reassurance. Minutes later, the lights came up to signal that the dance, and my brief introduction to intimacy, had ended.

That night, it was comforting to sit across the kitchen table from Mom and tell her only the positive highlights of my evening. I offered to demonstrate for my mother how I danced that night. She stood in the middle of the kitchen and extended her arms, one shoulder height, one waist high as she would await my dad to waltz her around a dancefloor. I stepped up to her and put my arms around her waist just as I had Andrea.

"Oh!" Mom gasped. "I didn't realize you danced like that."

When I had my arms around Andrea, her broad diameter left my hands meeting at the small of her back. With her, I simply wrapped one hand around my other and we danced. But my mom always had a tiny waist. When I put my arms around her, my arms met in the middle of my forearms, leaving my hands to dangle.

Mom pulled away from me suddenly. "You never, never touch a girl's behind when you dance with her!"

I didn't realize my fingers had grazed Mom's rear.

"I taught you to have more respect."

The disdain in her reprimand shocked me. Embarrassed, I raced to my bedroom. At the time, the pattern seemed obvious. The only salvation I knew was to hide.

I lay on my bed sensing a severed connection with my mother that made me miss her. It made no sense. She was only down the hall, but something felt as though I had lost her. As alone as I had felt outside my home, and in my head, I sensed a need to repair whatever I'd inadvertently damaged between my mother and me.

I slunk back to the kitchen repentantly. Stopping in the doorway I mumbled, "I'm sorry." I didn't know exactly what I was apologizing for. I think hearing my mother speak so gruffly to me after I'd striven my whole life to do whatever I thought would win her love scared me. I had intentionally severed ties with my friends for fear they would realize I was gay. I couldn't imagine damaging my relationship with my mother. But my next mistake seemed to have the exact effect I was hoping to avoid.

My mother hated sentimentality. Young as I was at this time, I sensed it even if I couldn't identify and articulate it. But emulating the kind of dramatic moment from television that resolved the conflict of an episode, I told my mother, "I know you didn't mean to snap at me. You're my mom. You love me, and I know you would never do anything to hurt me."

She sat there, silent. I think in part she was stunned by the sudden surge of emotion. What was I doing? I was a Leslie, and a Leslie did not express with actual words what we were feeling. My attempt to build a bridge only deepened the chasm of her reprimand.

Apparently having learned nothing from our last uncomfortable interaction, I retreated again to my bedroom. This time, thoughts infiltrated the territory just seconds earlier pulsating with emotion. Now I felt numb, but my mind raced with confusion. Did my big climactic speech convey how I truly perceived my mother? Or was it a grand, live TV moment that backfired? I don't remember coming back out of my room that night. I suppose I at least went into the bathroom to brush my teeth. I never went to sleep without brushing my teeth. But unlike every other night of my life, I don't remember going into the living room to say goodnight to my mom and dad. I crawled into bed feeling empty and confused. Ever since I was a toddler, I knew I would always be different from the rest of my family. That left me wondering who I really was, and who or what I would become. With all my sexual concerns and self-doubts, I could never pigeonhole myself like a flat character in a book. Yet I was sure I knew all my family members—clearly, predictably, and absolutely. My mother's reaction to my dance, and then her lack of response to my apology, threw into question what I thought I knew about them. All this time, I had perceived my family members as stable constants, and me an untethered question mark. Suddenly my mother was human to me. Even scarier, I entertained the possibility that she was also flawed.

At 14, I knew how much I still loved my mother. Although I had developed some self-reliance, I had not yet outgrown the vulnerability of needing her. During one strange, disconcerting interaction—perhaps because it included a rare physical connection—I acknowledged how little I really understood my mom.

If not she, then who was my foundation? When would the question mark I had become grow into a sturdy exclamation point declaring my identity?

This was my mother. Mom. Ma.

As a gay toddler, I looked to her as my role model. It was she, not my father, that I wanted to grow up to be like. She was my constant when Dad was away working. When we ran errands, she was my mentor, capitalizing on teachable moments with me—her open, hungry student.

I didn't know who she was. She had not suddenly changed. But in her abrupt reaction, and my Tennessee Williams Act III reply, I saw a gap between us that I'd previously never recognized. In that awkward, dramatic moment, I sensed that the question mark I was had landed, but not in my mother's paragraph. My story would be written somewhere else as I became a man who would not please my mother—or my father. Only time would confirm how deep was the chasm I feared separated who I really was from who they were willing to acknowledge. But my awakening began that night. Ironically, it was prompted by an intimate slow dance with a girl.

17

Building Hell

The summer after St. Linus, I had to find activities I could do alone. I watched plenty of television. I started writing fiction—first stories, then screenplays. I rode my bike. I took walks after dark with our dog Bonnie tugging excitedly on her leash. As I had every Saturday for years, I walked to Wise Owl Book Shoppe with the money I'd earned mowing my grandmothers' lawns to buy Rona Barrett's *Gossip* or *Hollywood* magazines or build my collection of movie tie-in novels.

As the summer lingered, I questioned the wisdom of remaining immersed in the distractions of watching television and reading. On one trek back from the bookstore, with the pungent nostril-burn of fresh ink wafting from the tabloid featuring a full-page photo of Stella Stevens, I scared myself thinking that the path I'd chosen left me lonely for now, and that if I persisted through adulthood, it signified my slow descent into madness. That was the last time I walked to Wise Owl.

Without my usual friends and familiar pop culture distractions, I was bored enough to give fear my full attention, especially during mass. As congregates sang and choreographed their way through traditional sitting, standing, and kneeling, I envisioned disappearing calendar pages. Each Sunday marked one week closer to the day I would face the unknown in high school—which terrified me. Renouncing my last friendship, I didn't have anyone to share my anxiety about the first major change I ever had to face. Because my sister and brother were several years older than I, they would not be at Divine Child High School when I started. I did not know what to expect. But, all too clearly, I did know I was embarking on a new chapter of my life entirely alone. Every Sunday, each "peace be with you" at church reminded me that, although outwardly I was sullen and depressed, inside torrential terror agitated me to nausea. Another Sunday. Another mass. Another step closer to the Wailing Wall.

Divine Child was a small high school. At freshman orientation the week before classes began, I learned that one central hallway formed a large square through the entire building. Except for my gym class, which was in an adjacent building, every classroom was off that hallway. Discovering I couldn't get physically lost didn't help. By the time I entered Divine Child, I was so emotionally and mentally lost I lumbered like a sad sloth through that hallway.

I started off my year at Divine Child High School completely wrong. Because DC was not in walking distance from our home like St. Linus, my brother Randy, who had not yet moved to East Lansing to attend Michigan State, drove me to school. I didn't sleep much the week leading up to that first day of school. I dressed that morning in a catatonic stupor—my head was hazy from sleeplessness and my chest ricocheted pangs of anxiety as if a panicked sharpshooter were defending himself by machine-gunning at flocks of attacking birds.

I met Randy at his Buick Skylark, in which we would drive to DC with the windows wide open and The New York Dolls blaring from his 8-track. Before we got in, he offered his big-brother advice. "You can't go to school like that."

I thought I was dressed wrong. I was, with way-too-loose baggy green corduroy slacks, a short sleeve shirt, and a sweater in hand because I didn't know if the school would be hot or cold, and I don't learn as well when I'm uncomfortable. But it wasn't my clothes that prompted Randy's advice. "Look what you're carrying."

I didn't think I'd need spiral notebooks for every class the first day, and I wouldn't get my textbooks until instruction started. So, I had a small tablet, a black ink pen (I liked writing in black better than blue), and a pencil in case my pen unexpectedly ran out of ink.

"You don't carry anything with you on the first day of school."

I stood outside his car not knowing how to reply. *What if the teacher tells us something I need to remember? How will I write it down?*

"You know what people are going to think of you if you walk into school the first day ready to learn?"

I had spent the entire summer feeling so terrified of adapting to a new school, I never once wondered what kind of impression I would make on anyone else. I was in survival mode—with no background or experience to tell me if I had any skills to face the challenge.

Though I could feel in his tone how lovingly he intended his advice, I just wasn't equipped in that moment to take it. My first day at a new school terrified me all summer. Learning I was already doing it wrong oscillated every buried anxiety. When younger, I might have feared a sudden moistening of my eyes, the ultimate betrayal of a weak and troubled gay boy. Now older and cowering at the back of my dark closet, I had no words, not even a thank-you for my brother. As an ironic saving grace, my baggy pants had deep pockets. I slid the tablet and writing implements into my right pocket because my left pocket was already filled with a small packet of tissues. I always carried tissues because of my ragweed allergies which, par for the course of this day, were the worst in late summer.

The left corner of Randy's mouth curled upward.

Yes, I thought, staring at him from the passenger side of his car, *This really is the best I can do*.

Randy always played his music so loud when he drove, I didn't have to worry about conversing on the way to school. He roared into the Divine Child parking lot as someone who had conquered this territory. He stopped the car at an angle from the building and pointed to a side door. "Go in that entrance. You don't want to go in the front door on the first day."

I had no idea why. Somehow Randy had mastered a set of social rules that I didn't know existed and couldn't imagine why they mattered.

"And ditch the sweater, Rog." He yanked it out of my hand and tossed it into the back seat. With nothing to grip, I curled my hands into sweat-petrified fists and headed to the door Randy recommended. When I turned to wave goodbye, the taillights of his Skylark seemed to be squinting at me.

Heaven and Hell
(AKA English and Gym)

I didn't realize how shy I could be until I started high school. Maybe because I knew all my classmates at St. Linus since first grade, I could be quiet in my grade school classes without feeling self-conscious. As a sack of insecurity throughout my freshman year, I kept loading it until my 100-pound frame felt like one of those huge boulders being dragged uphill by slaves to form The Pyramids.

The first interaction I had with any classmate at DC began when a skinny kid with curly, already-receding hair said, "Like those pants."

My initial reaction was to smile gratefully. But when he followed his compliment with a glance toward his surrounding buddies, who all laughed, I realized he was only making an impression on them at my expense.

Days later in algebra, the guy in front of me passed back a worksheet and started talking to me as if I were somebody else. When he finally turned, he stopped short. "Oh, it's you. Big nose. That story wasn't for you." Then he turned around and never spoke to me again.

I felt so emotionally vapid in my new high school, I didn't even know how to care. These people were strangers to me, or rather, I perceived myself as a stranger to them. Although probably only 70% of the students attending Divine Child High School had transitioned from Divine Child Grade School on the same church property, I held the perception that I was the only piece of this puzzle that didn't fit. Because I thought I didn't know how to communicate with any of my classmates, I simply lumped them all together as lifelong friends in a community where I didn't belong. Much of that belief came from my gay sensibility that told me I was the only person in the world exactly like me.

All that first semester, I felt increasingly depressed every single morning having to return to a school where I remained emotionally numb. My one consolation: I found some comfort in familiarity. Once I learned the routines of my classes, I focused on my studies, in which I'd more than made up for my sixth-grade descent into academic mediocrity. I had no idea how to improve my vacuous social lot, especially because I was determined to keep secret who I really was and how I felt.

Once I knew where all my classes were, I found routes to get to each more efficiently so I never risked being outpaced by the tardy bell. Although the school had only one major hallway that led to all the classrooms, I could time how quickly I shot out of one room to make progress toward another to avoid hallway congestion. With no concern about having to end a conversation with anyone, the goal provided little emotional peaks throughout the day. It gave me something to anticipate as each class ended.

I started the day with my favorite subject, English. To my dismay, it was taught by a coach who cared nothing about literature. We read biographies like *The Babe Ruth Story*, and took vocabulary tests every Friday. After Randy left for college, Judy drove me to school every morning. But she worked downtown, which left me to walk home every afternoon. I spent Mondays memorizing all my vocabulary for the test on Friday. On the way home on Thursdays, I'd review every word, part of speech, and definition I'd learned. With over a mile to cover—often in the snow which required me to walk slower—I challenged myself to recite them all with 100% accuracy without looking at my workbook before I reached our driveway.

Even though I didn't read any good literature in class that year, my love of movies led me to imagine myself directing and acting out every part in the movies I was writing in my head. One plot involved two teenage boys stranded like the characters in *Lord of the Flies*, a book I read in eighth grade with a teacher who did like literature. But instead of being isolated by a plane crash, these boys were kidnapped and put in an underground bomb shelter. In the cold of winter as I put on my own gloves, stuffed fat with fleece padding for the Michigan cold, I imagined filming the close-up of my hand slipping into the sleek leather gloves of the kidnapper determined not to leave fingerprints.

As I developed their characterizations, the boys mirrored my own personality—studious, shy, and more comfortable with orderly scholastic pursuits than the sloppiness of sports or parties. Around this time, I started entertaining thoughts of suicide. Instead of acting on them, I filtered them through the hopeless, trapped characters in my screenplay. Having them both die in this isolation was definitely a plausible conclusion.

But I considered alternate plot possibilities. Without the gloves on, I imagined one boy first awakening to his attraction for the other. That young bare hand—my young bare hand—reached forward to touch the cheek of the other boy, who responded with a relieved smile to discover that his secret thoughts were not only shared, but being acted upon by the first.

In the script I only wrote in my head, I imagined the stage direction indicating that the first young boy "goes gay," as if his realization only occurred because of the imprisonment of forced closeness. In my mind, the outside world was too expansive to imagine happening upon, or even discovering through effort, that any other young man could be thinking or feeling as I was then.

My extended walk home nurtured my creative imaginings, but my English class did not. It was in a small classroom with two rows of desks facing a mirror image of another two rows of desks. Mr. Bognar often assigned us silent reading while he sat at his desk grading papers or reading a newspaper inconspicuously folded inside his gradebook. I don't remember anyone in that class except Mr.

Bognar, a rather attractive 30-something with blond bangs whose slowly paced sentences allowed him to enunciate each word. It was not an affectation of an overly conscientious English teacher, but a result of what must have been an oversized palate.

He was the first male teacher I ever had. I felt the same desire to make a good impression on him as I did on my uncles. For me, it was a blessing Mr. Bognar taught this first-period subject I loved and excelled in most enthusiastically. In fifth period, he became Coach Bognar of my gym class. I never liked being a sports spectator, and except for one season of T-ball, was never forced to play them. St. Linus School didn't have a gym, so our only exercise came after nuns yelled for us to quit loitering in the halls at recess and get outside for some of God's fresh air.

If even a non-literary English class offered a few heavenly reading opportunities, after-lunch gym was my idea of Hell. I didn't like having to change clothes in a locker room with other boys. I was shy and self-conscious and had no prurient interest in even catching a glimpse of males my own age. The toilet stalls had no doors (at a very naïve 14 years of age, I had no clue why the doors had to be removed), and one student with an apparently quick metabolism went right from lunch to disrobing at his locker to sitting on the pot and taking a loud dump every single day. I couldn't imagine how he could do that in front of other people. Most of the time, I held even my urine until I could go home to pee behind the locked door of our bathroom.

Those brief but consistent locker room visits made me realize how out-of-sync I was with other boys my age. In some ways, overhearing their conversations left me doubly attuned to how socially inept I was. Music would play loudly, and boys would make cracks about lyrics. When Frankie Valli sang "My eyes adored you, though I never laid a hand on you," some boy scoffed, "Yeah, I'll bet." This sweet song spoke to a romantic idealism I thought at the time I would never realize, so I felt particularly incensed by the crassness of his comment. Few of my peers seemed to share my sentiment, for most laughed or made sucking noises one might hear at a construction site when a leggy woman passed.

Other guys talked about what parties they would attend that weekend, and some even discussed which brand of beer was their favorite. Not only did I not attend (or get invited to) parties, but I also almost never talked to any of my classmates throughout the school day.

I felt humiliated having to dress out in shorts and run laps around the basketball court. I resented every silly game Coach Bognar made us play. He would divide us into small teams that alternated time on the court. During stick hockey, I ran a lot—as far away from the puck as I could. I focused on two objectives: staying on the opposite side of the gym from the action and waiting for the coach's whistle to end my misery.

Finally, his whistle blared. But then he hollered, "Leslie, stay out there."

I was too self-conscious to resent Coach Bognar for making me play. I know I wasn't the worst athlete in class. I even surprised myself by having more natural ability than I ever imagined. But I was so determined not to support this nightmare graduation requirement that I dug in my heels and did as little as possible.

Once coach created a volleyball tournament of four teams. My team captain was a decent athlete and rival with the best athlete in class—the guy who took a dump every day as we dressed out in the locker room. During our game, I stood amid the middle of my teammates, not at the net, and not at the back. I also stood close enough to other guys so that somebody, *somebody* would surely go after the ball if it came our way. Sure enough, the volleyball sailed in our direction. I curled my fist in defiance, not realizing that it was the very clenching of volleyball players preparing to make their move.

I didn't. I stood there and let the ball drop at my feet. I know it was selfish, but I didn't care. I had to do my time in this class to get through high school, but I wasn't being graded for effort, simply for not missing more than 10 school days a semester.

My team captain put his face right into mine. Until that time, I don't think I'd ever been that physically close to anyone except my parents or grandmothers when they hugged me goodnight as a very small child. The red rage in his cheeks looked all the more crimson framed by his blond hair. He shook like a jackhammer. His pupils seared with fury.

I have never been in a physical fight, so I didn't even know signs of impending violence. If I had, I might have reacted defensively to the menacing curl of his fists. But he wasn't priming for attack. Instead, he balled his hands and gestured how to return the ball over the net. Through gritted teeth he spat, "When the ball comes to you, you *hit* the ball," he made the motion again. "*Hit* the ball."

His fireball intensity was no match for my dull indifference. I had no confidence in my physical abilities, and even less interest in participating in this hellishness. I just wanted to finish this class with a passing grade so I never had to suffer through the slow execution of this testosterone-pumping chaos.

I thought I didn't care what the other boys in class thought of me, and my stoic indifference to my volleyball team captain's acidic reaction reinforced the thought. Initially, I liked feeling invisible. But one day that perspective changed. Every class period we started by sitting on the gym floor in rows far enough apart to complete warmup exercises. I was the last kid in the last row. I liked that the guy in front of me had sprouted prematurely. His Goliath frame, even when he was seated or doing sit-ups, hid me from Coach Bognar and blocked my view of most of my classmates.

One class period Coach Bognar had rearranged the order of our rows. As usual, mentally I was barely present, probably working through snags in the latest screenplay I was developing on my walks home. I stepped to my usual spot for roll call and warmups, not noticing that I was in the wrong row. Before the last boys filtered in from the locker room, the tall student slipped toward me and whispered, "Our row's over there now. You can stay with me."

I didn't know the student's name. After his instruction to me I paid attention during roll call to learn who he was. The gentle kindness of his gesture left me a little smitten. Until that day, I only knew he existed because he shielded me from Coach Bognar's view, and potential criticism. It didn't occur to me until then that invisibility is a reciprocal perspective. I responded to my feeling invisible to them by making them invisible to me. For the rest of my days at Divine Child, I hated the class a little less because I looked forward to seeing the guy in front of me. He was no Goliath after all, but a Samson whose real strength was kindness. He wasn't that handsome, but what fourteen-year-old is, even to another fourteen-year-old? But his simple, sweet consideration made him so attractive to me I sometimes fantasized about him at night. Fantasizing about someone I knew, and my own age, was a new phenomenon for me. Despite how idealized and romantic the thoughts were, I never considered revealing them to anyone, especially him.

19

The Wages of Sin

It wasn't until spring semester that I fully appreciated why I could never reveal my true feelings to anyone. Once a semester, the school offered mini seminars on a variety of different topics that could help students develop new personal interests, or perhaps introduce them to subjects that might later inspire a career direction. This far into my year, I was still depressed and numb, but at least distracted as I developed screenplays in my head. For those screenplays, I started observing my peers, if only to determine how their individual personality traits would flesh out the characters I was developing with more complexity in my plots. This mixed-up Monday of going anywhere to learn anything left me sleepless with anxiety the weekend preceding it.

That morning our first period class served as a short homeroom session. Mr. Bognar passed out little booklets that described each course, what teacher would be leading it, and in which classroom. I looked for a creative writing session. None. I searched for a movie appreciation course. None. I didn't care about anything they were teaching. But then I saw a pattern. All the teachers were offering their workshops in their own classrooms. So, no matter what the topic, I determined to follow my daily schedule, going to my usual first to eighth period classrooms, and attend whatever session they offered. If I didn't like the topic, I could spend my time observing new students, from all four grade levels, and take characterization notes for my current screenplay.

I don't remember what Mr. Bognar taught because it was something about sports. Although I didn't pay attention to what he said that mini-seminar, I benefitted from having stayed for his session. Apparently impressed by my effort to at least expand my academic understanding of sports, Coach Bognar subsequently was more patient with me in fifth period, while Mr. Bognar took greater advantage of my love of reading in first. Each morning, he called on me to carry the discussions about the literary-limited books he made us read. They weren't brilliant novels or even stellar nonfiction, but I could talk about any book or movie in ways I could never talk about anything that would reveal who I really was, or what I felt emotionally or sexually.

But feel it I did during the second period special sessions day. It brought an epiphany that clarified for me why I dropped my St. Linus friends and hunkered invisibly through Divine Child. My usual second period class was French I with Sister Cynthia, a lively young nun with a broad mouth and one diagonal cascade of strawberry blonde bangs covering her forehead. Most every morning, Sister Cynthia was loud and overtly frustrated that we French I students didn't show more enthusiasm by matching her Fourth of July sparkler energy. I recall one morning I was feeling so strangled by depression I couldn't even speak. When she called on me to answer a question in French, I wasn't even able to reply in English. I pretended to search for the answer in my brain, all the while hating the focus she was drawing to me while I was feeling so black and vulnerable. Finally, I offered a tiny nod and shrug to suggest I had tried to come up with her answer, but couldn't.

Instead of moving on to another student, she closed in on me by coming right up to my desk and pounding her palm several times on it. "Come on, Rogie Baby, you can do this."

I stopped breathing. If I exhaled my emotions might rise to the surface and betray me in front of all my classmates. I didn't know why I felt so dark this day in particular, but I wanted to be anywhere at that moment that could free me from Sister Cynthia's direct, expectant gaze. When my stiff dullness persisted, she turned with dismissive frustration. Like a Shakespeare aside, said to no one but intended for every observer to hear, she shot, "You people have no idea how hard it is to teach freshmen. God what I wouldn't give for a morning full of upperclassmen." Her delivery of that last line suggested that she wasn't talking to God but using the word as a dramatic expletive.

She got her wish the day of the mini seminars because her attendees were mostly juniors and seniors. From my usual second-period desk, I watched Sister Cynthia flit among only the older students. At one point, she even sat on a desktop, crossed her feet and swung them like an overwound clock pendulum as she regaled the cluster of seniors with her funny story.

I had never before sat quietly in the presence of even these slightly older students, but I liked it. Though brief, the opportunity helped me appreciate Sister Cynthia's frustration with freshmen. These students did seem to relate to Sister Cynthia with a much more cordial dynamic than the big teacher/little students veil that separated the adult from us children like a confessional screen. I sensed a natural human closeness that peeled the scab of my self-imposed withdrawal with a shock of pain. I was tired of feeling lonely.

I don't know if that awareness preceded or followed the observation that nestled into my soul that day, but the pivotal character in this memory was not Sister Cynthia, but a student whose name I've never known, and who I don't recall ever seeing again except during that 40-minute session on a topic about which I paid no attention. When the young Sister visited with individual students—working the room, I suppose, now that she felt in her element with an audience of mostly more mature students—she stopped in front of the desk of a burly male who laughed at her comment. This senior guy, likely a star football player because he wore his letter jacket in class, was not traditionally handsome. My Hollywood magazines set that standard with images of Robert Redford as dapper Jay Gatsby, or Paul Newman and Steve McQueen with strategic soot splatters from battling a towering inferno.

This senior was a more familiarly pale Midwestern teen with large-rimmed glasses. This special day also allowed students to dress more casually. Perhaps his faded jeans and tan suede Chukkas made him less intimidating to me than he might have been in a starched white shirt and tie. I only know that when he laughed in response to Sister's story, the warmth of his open smile washed over me, and I was momentarily infatuated. But the ecstatic physical and emotional surge of my fascination collapsed like Samson's temple when a thought that defined this stage of my life transformed what could have been a crush into crushing damnation.

If he knew what I was thinking, I told myself, *he would hate me.*

I had associated my feelings of affection—and they were affection, not just lust—with an anticipated response, dark and loathing. It was no wonder I was drowning in the mire of loneliness and had found as escapes the beautiful men of movies and television and a fascination with writing that would allow me to create a world I assumed did not exist. As I saw my life, I would never have the love, or even the honest human connection, that everybody else could take for granted.

20

Surprising Connections

Sometimes during that first semester at Divine Child I never spoke a word the entire day at school. In third period Introduction to Art class, Mr. Foye played his radio on days we were left alone to create whatever he taught us the day before. I watched a slender redhead bounce around to Elton John singing "Island Girl" and wondered what she had to be so happy about.

In my last two classes of the day, I saw another person who never seemed to talk to anyone. She was a blonde who sat across the room in seventh period religion and in the desk right behind me in eighth period algebra. Before each class started and the second a lecture ended, she pulled out a novel and resumed reading. Most of the books were paperbacks as thick as Leon Uris's *QBVII*. She tore through several novels per week. Perhaps other students unlike us would find her literary consumption sad. I was impressed by how smart she must be.

Even so young, I was rarely attracted to boys my own age. The best-looking freshman—a blond junior varsity football player—was, predictably, very popular. Not overly muscular, he had broad shoulders that rounded at the end of very long, bulging trapezius muscles. He must have known they were among his best features because when girls flirted with him, he tilted his head to grin.

He was the most confident freshmen at DC. Dressed out and waiting on the basketball court floor for gym class to begin, he would recline onto one elbow and tell the guy next to him, "This is my *Playgirl* pose." Then he'd laugh as if he were just kidding about how beautiful he knew he was to the opposite sex. I'd never seen a naked male centerfold, but I knew about them. In my fan magazines, Rona Barrett often mentioned Burt Reynolds' *Cosmopolitan* photoshoot.

One time the poser sat next to me at a pep rally. It must have honored varsity upperclassmen exclusively because the cute blond was not a featured athlete. Somehow, he ended up at one of the high, obscure bleachers where I hid because I only attended pep rallies under duress.

All around us, students were jumping and hollering and cheering. Even at age 14, I was confounded by their behavior. In moments I wasn't feeling too overwhelmed and annoyed to even think, I wondered, *When are these people going to grow out of this?*

At one point in the pep rally, somebody announced that a special guest had arrived to lead the excitement.

Excitement? That's not what I was calling it.

One of the coaches from the University of Michigan eyeing potential recruits from DC came to the mic. The crowd roared.

From someone who worked for a college, I expected wisdom and inspiration. Instead, he asked everyone to stand and chant with him, at the top of their voices, "We hate Ohio State! We hate Ohio State!"

I didn't stand. The irony of this chant made me smile. I imagined my dad, inflated with pride, having paid exorbitant tuition to give us a good moral upbringing at a school whose entire student body was, in unison, screaming their hate for an entire institution of higher learning—or at least their athletes.

It's quite likely I never smiled at Divine Child until that moment. But my reaction to the inanity of all these religious leaders and students chanting hate struck me as ludicrous. Smiling at my own macabre thought, I turned to my right to notice that someone else had not stood up and chanted either. It was the *Playgirl* blond. With a lingering gaze fixed on me, he returned my grin. Except for the trapezius tilt, it was the same look he gave when flirting.

My smile still frozen, I stared at him. He kept his eyes locked on mine. I wondered what he thought. I questioned whether he was grinning at me or with me. My inclination was to assume he was judging me somehow, but his smile was too gentle.

At the time, it never occurred to me that he might be attracted to me. With my forlorn self-concept, I believed I was the only young man in the world attracted to other men.

I never concluded anything substantive from that glance, which ended when all the Ohio State haters sat back down around us. But sharing a smile with so handsome a young man filled me with the same gratitude I felt for my gym class Samson. Ironically, the two positive connections I made with male peers at that school happened in the gym, where I was most miserable.

In winter, I started thinking about acting on, rather than writing about, my suicidal thoughts when my dad announced that we were moving . . . to Texas. My first thought: *Big deal. So I'll have four other walls to stare at.* But when the reality of moving began to crystallize, I felt hope. We were moving 1,400 miles away. This was my chance to start over.

By this time, though woeful in social development, I had mastered academics. We moved in April, a full nine weeks before the end of the school year. On my last day at Divine Child, I had to get all my teachers to fill in a grid indicating my current grade for the class.

English   A

French   A

Art/Music Appreciation   A

Lunch

PE   Passing
                    (*Halleluiah, it's over*)

Physical Science

Religion   A

Algebra

The last two teachers I found standing together: Mr. Carroll, my handsome algebra teacher, and Sister Cecilia, who had to fill in my physical science grade. Mr. Carroll wrote "A," shook my hand, and wished me good luck in

Houston. Sister Cecilia kept looking back and forth between her gradebook and my sign-out sheet.

"You know, you're really between an A and A-," she told me.

Mr. Carroll came to my defense. "You're kidding. Look at his grades. You'd really give him an A-?"

She gave me an A.

I felt affirmed. I thought Mr. Carroll barely knew me. Now this handsome man acknowledged my accomplishment, and even encouraged another teacher to let me leave with a perfect grade point.

After seventh period religion class, Miss Croskey called me to her desk and handed me a present. I unwrapped a copy of *Jonathan Livingston Seagull*. She gave me her address and told me to write when I arrived in Texas.

Again, I was stunned. I knew Miss Croskey liked me, but she liked all her students. Her gift and offer to correspond made me think I had no idea my potential impact on other people.

Last period of the day, I surprised myself by feeling emotional. After months of thinking I was lost and disconnected from everyone, I grew sentimental. Less than a year earlier, I gazed at the empty hallway of St. Linus through a steel diamond of the accordion gate and realized a piece of my life was forever behind me. This time, I sat in Mr. Carroll's algebra class for the last time knowing I would never make a peer connection at Divine Child if I didn't right now.

When Mr. Carroll ended his lecture, I turned around. The blonde reader behind me was already into her book.

"Today's my last day," I told her.

She looked up.

"I'm moving to Texas."

She dog-eared her page and gave me her full attention. "Are you excited?"

I knew I was hopeful about making a new start. But excited? "Yes," I realized, "I am."

Fran Cyburt wrote her name and address on a corner of a notebook page, tore it off and handed it to me. "Write me when you get to Texas."

"Hi, Fran." I didn't know her name until I read it. She had the handwriting of a confident artist. "I'm Roger."

Fran smiled. "I thought it was Leslie . . . from roll call." Until he memorized our names, Mr. Carroll did call attendance the first few weeks of class. "No, Leslie is my last name. My first is Roger."

She extended her hand. "Well hello, Roger Leslie."

Shaking hands physically reinforced a connection.

The bell rang. My last class at DC was over.

Fran gathered her books. I'd already turned mine in.

"Do write me," she encouraged. "I promise to write back."

"I will."

I left Divine Child having a potential friend.

With Fran's address as the bookmark I used in Miss Croskey's gift of *Jonathan Livingston Seagull*, I packed for Texas, this time feeling free of my past rather than afraid of my future.

Because of my grades, I didn't have to finish my freshman year in Texas. My summer vacation that year began in early April and didn't end until after Labor Day. With hope for beginning a new life, and already having survived the crippling fear of starting a new school once, I capitalized on the opportunity to savor the entire bicentennial summer and adjust to Texas' swelter.

Instead of developing new screenplays those first months in Houston, I corresponded with family back home. First, I shared with my grandmothers details of our trip south. When I wrote a similar letter to extended family, my mother's reaction surprised me. She wanted to read everything I told them before mailing my letters, and sometimes suggested deleting details. I didn't think I was sharing anything personal, so her insistence about serving as my editor struck me as odd.

Rather than let her censor my writing, I quit sending letters to those relatives and focused on corresponding with Miss Croskey and Fran. I shared with my former teacher how Jonathan Livingston Seagull's tenacity inspired me. I especially liked that he dismissed the naysayers among his flock to answer the call of his own ambitions. That was exactly what I intended to do as I started my new life. She sent a lovingly teacher-y reply filled with kind encouragement. After we finished sharing mutual admiration about the book, our correspondence lost momentum. I don't know who stopped writing first, but those letters ended during my sophomore year.

Fran surprised me. I knew I would keep my promise to write. But honestly, I expected her to send me a "well, good luck with your new life" reply, and that would be the end of it. Really, I was fine with that prospect. The gift of hope she gave me those last few minutes at Divine Child really was enough for me to feel forever grateful.

I wrote Fran a short but newsy letter. Very quickly, she replied with one a bit longer, sharing basic biographical information about her immediate family. I replied in kind. It was her next letter that set the foundation for our friendship. Perhaps because I was 1,400 miles away, where her news would have no repercussions, she poured her heart out. She shared frustrations concerning some domestic issues happening around her, and thus affecting her and how she perceived her entire family dynamic.

At age 15, I didn't really know what to reply, but in every line of her letter, I sensed her desire for an immediate, compassionate, and understanding response. At the time, I imagined her feeling so embarrassed about bearing the soul of her entire family that she might never write again. But dependable as ever, she replied promptly. The new letter began with gratitude for my considerate reply. What followed impressed me even more than her courage for opening the vein to reveal the pulse of her family. She expanded on the original story, this time from a more unemotional perspective.

Although her family saga focused on her frustration with what she considered a flaw, I responded more to what I read between the lines. Her family, or at least she, did not shrink from openly identifying and exploring what she considered her family's life-shaping domestic issues. At that age, I never knew to look far enough outside of myself to understand that, while being gay may have been unique in my immediate family, my decision to conceal the problem rather than expose and explore it rationally continued a design etched into my family crest. The pattern was so consistent, it never occurred to me to respond to her opening up about her issues by sharing the sexual secret I brought with me to Texas.

21

Experiencing My Ideal

My first weeks in Texas, I joined the CYO—Catholic Youth Organization—at our new church, St. Matthew's. During the meetings, I was touched by a spiritual curiosity more intellectual than emotional. Our discussions made me appreciate the impact of my long-term, consistent religious education. St. Matthew's didn't have a school, so all the other CYO members studied religion and faith and morality only at these informal gatherings. Group leader, earthy Mrs. Whitworth and her cohort, a younger broad-hipped woman named Stacy Donovan who wore stretch polyester slacks and striped poncho tops, were valiant teachers. Beyond lectures, they even engaged in role-playing for us. In one scene, Stacy pretended to be a teen who had to tell her none-too-pleased mother, played by Mrs. Whitworth, that she was pregnant.

They went full out, with Stacy crying and Mrs. Whitworth responding first by lambasting her daughter, and then ultimately discussing with her the issue and consequences of her actions. Afterward, they would lead the eight or so CYO teens in a group forum about the context of their skits. Each season, they covered different social and personal issues. The topic of homosexuality never arose.

Although I didn't really learn much in these CYO sessions, they helped make me aware that Mom and Dad availed me to a rigorous spiritual education. My daily religion courses in Michigan invited deeper, consistent examinations of God and spirituality. When I shared any insight I had learned from my Catholic school teachers— including Sister James Marie—I discovered that repeating what I'd heard them say led me to develop my own ideas about faith—sometimes consistent with their lesson, sometimes an extension of it, and often at odds with it. By age 16, I recognized how essential spiritual exploration was to my self-image. Without noticing how or when it happened, I became a young man of faith.

I didn't sense instant salvation. My new faith couldn't promise I was saved from Hell, or earn my place in the arms of Jesus the way born-again Sister Gert had prodded me to beg. But it saved my life because, as a teen who knew I was gay, it kept me from re-indulging those old thoughts of suicide. My faith brought some comfort, but not enough strength to break me out of emotional hiding. It was a lonely but not entirely awful space, as it cultivated creative imagination and deepened my resolve to resume writing once I started my sophomore year at Jersey Village High School.

Second period English II with Miss Adele McClendon immediately became my favorite class. Perhaps because this course contrasted so sharply with the oh-so-non-literary English I at Divine Child, I became enraptured by the writing and literature and critical analysis of different forms and genres of fiction and nonfiction.

Miss McClendon was low key and intelligent. She wore large plastic-rimmed glasses that barely stayed suspended on her flat nose, and she was shaped like a bell. Unlike most teachers, she would occasionally share personal details of her life to broaden and deepen the literary lesson. She let us know she was single and had a cat. One time while discussing a character with unique spiritual powers, she led into her confession by insisting, "If you tell anybody I said this, I'll say you lied . . ." and then she shared how, while driving one day, she got a spiritual gut-punch about her cat. When she arrived home, she found her cat collapsed on her floor with a broken leg.

In the 1970s, Texas adopted an open-concept of teaching. The entire English department met in a huge, cavernous wing where as many as eight classes could be going on simultaneously, in earshot of one another. Occasionally hearing other teachers and their students made me appreciate Miss McClendon even more. She was sharp, and she engaged us in class discussions that freed me to drop my self-consciousness to become immersed in literary exploration. I never worried about opening up in this class and expressing thoughts and feelings about every work of literature we read. In her class, I felt the happiest and most confident I had since starting high school.

Besides reading novels such as *A Separate Peace*, we studied plays and movies. Analyzing films in class revived my love of cinema. Movies no longer felt like mere escape, but tools for becoming a better writer. During our first Christmas break in Texas, I saw *Network* and *Rocky*. I especially loved *Network* and was awed by the scathing audacity of Chayefsky's writing. How it contrasted with the poignancy of his earlier teleplay *Marty*, another movie with writing that moved and inspired me. I also loved the character Rocky, who struck me as a Jonathan Livingston Seagull in the boxing ring. I left that movie wanting to become the Rocky of young writers.

Back at school, Miss McClendon told me she had seen that film, too.

"What did you think?"

"I liked it. But they certainly stacked everything in the world they could to make you want to root for Rocky. I think the only thing they left out was a dying Jewish mother." Her commentary intrigued me and taught me how people can perceive the same work very differently.

For Christmas that year, Randy bought me a book of the David Newman/Robert Benton script of *Bonnie and Clyde* that included liner notes from director Arthur Penn and a collection of commentary on the movie nearly ten years after its release. In an effort to find my own voice, I strove to write a poem about Bonnie and Clyde different from the one Bonnie Parker wrote about the Barrow Gang.

I found the courage to start sharing my writing. I gave that poem to Miss McClendon, not as an assignment, but as a first step to starting my writing career. Although the poem did not hint at any secrets about myself that I wanted to remain hidden, sharing my work with her left me vulnerable but excited.

Her kind but tentative review of my writing sent a clear message: I had potential but needed to develop my talent. It made me hunger to improve.

One of my favorite classmates was very Southern, fun-loving Roxanne Herrin. She had layers of long brown hair, was quick to laugh, and her voice carried so loud and long through the English wing, students in other classes turned to see what was so funny. One day she felt cold, so I let her wear my blue corduroy jacket. It wasn't a romantic gesture, but an act of kindness that made me feel so much more connected to my peers than I even knew how at Divine Child.

Another student in that class, Mindy Dover, had scoliosis. She needed back surgery mid-year, so during her last class session with us that year, Miss McClendon gave her a "Best of Luck and Get Well Soon" party. We were all to bring a little present, and Miss McClendon reminded us to keep the tone of the party upbeat. Mindy had a painful operation and difficult recovery ahead of her.

For the party, Miss McClendon moved us to a small, enclosed meeting room behind the library. Instead of sitting at rows of tables, we formed a circle with our chairs.

I ended up sitting beside another male student I didn't know but had noticed the previous semester. Facially, he was not very good looking, but as an athlete, he exuded a powerful masculinity. Perhaps because he wasn't so handsome, he was shy, which I found very attractive. It surprised me to discover how much primal pleasure I felt just sitting next to him. I was usually tongue-tied around guys I was attracted to, but in the warm atmosphere created by the private gathering, I initiated what turned out to be a very natural and congenial conversation. Accustomed to males dismissing me, I felt my tenderness for him mounting simply because we were engaged in a warm, respectful exchange. For the first time, I felt like a male peer's equal.

At the time it was the closest I could get to experiencing my ideal. I felt respected and liked by a fellow male even as I sensed my body prickling with attraction for him. At the time I was only beginning to imagine that maybe there were other young men in the world who felt as I did. I never suspected this classmate was among them. But I left Mindy's party believing in the possibility I might one day meet a kind young and gentle man who felt about me as I felt about him.

Alone among My Tribe

Around this same time, I started realizing some celebrities were gay. The ones I could identify never attracted me. Glittery Liberace would say on TV that he had not yet met the right woman, and so showered his mother with love and gifts. Rip Taylor played up his wispy mannerisms as unthreatening comedy under a mop of a toupee and fluttering fog of confetti. During this era, these were the kinds of men that people would talk about as gay.

During lunch my sophomore year, I sat at a table with three senior ROTC cadets. They were the first table of students I found to join when I started at my new school, and I was grateful they welcomed me. I didn't relate to them or their topics of conversation, so I rarely talked during lunch. On many days in Miss McClendon's class, I felt as though I was working my way skillfully out of my secretive cocoon.

Then every lunch period, I'd reclaim hints of the depression that consumed me at Divine Child.

Near the end of one lunch, the most outgoing of the students, and the only female, asked me if I was okay.

"Yes," I lied.

"You're so quiet."

"I'm fine."

"I don't believe you."

Stunned, I didn't reply.

"People as quiet as you aren't happy. What are you hiding?"

In a flash, my face burned. I hoped I hadn't turned red, but I was mortified that she would even ask.

Straight-faced, she bore her gaze into mine. My heart raced as my mind searched for a convincing denial.

Abruptly, her mouth sprang into a broad smile. "Join in the conversation sometime. You probably have something interesting to say."

The fear that flared through me suddenly drained out of me. It was a good thing I'd finished eating, because I had to race to the restroom to pee. When I got over the fear of wondering if she suspected I was gay, I decided she really was just being kind. The rest of the year, when they talked about topics other than war and science, I did make an effort to contribute to their conversations.

At lunch my junior year, I sat with a group so large they pushed two tables together to make room for all of us. Students from multiple grade levels sat in this cluster, including Richard Paul, a junior like me, and his younger sister, Renata.

From the beginning, I was intentionally conversant. But one time, the conversation left me speechless.

"Two guys moved into the house behind us," Renata giggled. "We think they're gay."

I froze.

"The fatter guy goes to work every day. The other one stays home. I guess that one's the wife."

Everybody else snickered.

I didn't yet have the courage to speak up, but I did have enough not to join in the laughter.

Always, I was attuned to who seemed gay and how people responded to them. In my sophomore biology class, Tim Whitfield was a fun, outgoing choir member who loved gossip. Hilariously, he could impersonate the worst singers in choir searching note-for-bad-note for their song's uncaptured pitch. He was wildly expressive, and I admired how "out" he seemed until, one day, he came to biology talking about his new girlfriend. Even more discouraging to me, all the classmates who avoided him before now praised and embraced him for finally being normal.

In my American history class was the most flamboyant guy I'd ever seen. Jeffrey Fortson had a huge afro, wore his nails as long as Barbra Streisand, and posed rather than just sat at his table. His aggressive body language demanded he not to be disturbed, and even the teacher respected it by never calling on him. I couldn't imagine how difficult his life at school must have been, but Jeffrey was never bullied, so far as I could tell. Impressively, a large group of Black female volleyball players protected him like a baby brother. While changing classes, he didn't seem to socialize with them, but they surrounded him like Secret Service.

Recognizing other gay people among my peers felt both reassuring and threatening. Finally, I knew I was not the only gay guy in my daily world. But I also felt no connection to the obviously gay students. That awareness no longer made me question if I was gay. But it kept me believing I was still entirely alone.

The Cry Room

In the darkness of my bedroom, I prayed every night, sometimes just to have somebody to talk to. I had long since abandoned the rote Catholic prayers connected with mass and the rosary. Instead, I began a one-sided dialog with God. In the silence of my own head, I talked to God. Occasionally I'd listen for a response in my soul.

The deadening silence during my pauses depressed me. I continued talking, working through what I was thinking (too much), what I was feeling (not much), and what those two distinct factions of my psyche were saying about who I was. When I talked to God in those attitudes, my one-sided dialogs were analytical and emotionless. Over time, they stopped helping. I needed to do something more. So I made a new commitment to get more out of church.

When I got my driver's license as a sophomore, Dad let me drive the two of us to St. Matthew's on Sunday mornings. No matter what season, it was always cold in the church. During mass, the huge vertical slats of the air conditioning vents rattled and sweated. Even in the suffocating humidity of Houston summers, I carried a sweater into the sanctuary so I wouldn't shiver the entire service.

Once I bought my own car, Mom helped me find a job as a sacker at Eagle Grocery Store beside the savings and loan where she was a bank teller. After promoting me to stocker, the manager often scheduled me to work early Sunday morning shifts before the store opened. That left only one mass time I could attend: 6:00 am. I started going to church alone.

My best moments in church did not come during mass, but afterward. After mass ended and most everyone filed out of the church, I hungered for something deeper and more meaningful. I'd slip into the interior "cry room," literally called that because parents were supposed to sit in there with their infant children so any errant crying wouldn't interrupt the mass. Those families could see the mass in progress through a large picture window facing the sacristy but heard the priest through a one-way intercom.

This small catacomb that could accommodate about twenty people was insulated by carpeting and thick upholstered seats of rich burgundy. Alone in this space, I felt something sad and helpless in me want to surrender to a greater power I hoped had answers that eluded me. Perhaps in part because I had set in my mind so young that I would be alone with my true desires this entire lifetime, one Sunday I fell in love with the idea of Jesus.

Instead of a judgmental God, Jesus symbolized a new truth: everyone, even I, was a beloved child of God. Like every other human being, I inherited that beautiful legacy. Consequently, my sexuality did not make me a Hell-bound exception to spiritual love. If in this world I would never find real intimacy with another man, the promise of something so idyllic in the spiritual realm infused my sweeping hopelessness with a ray of possibility. Maybe I really could continue the rest of my life without the human love I wanted if I could have it spiritually.

This revelation did not start me considering the priesthood. By this time, I was finding mass very unfulfilling, and noticing that my own spiritual values (and spiritual value) felt at odds with the tenets of the religion of my youth. I still didn't imagine I could find an interpersonal context for my spiritual growth. But I kept going deeper within, hoping that spiritual growth could replace the need for social development. Life soon smacked that hope right out of me.

No Rite of Passage

During Christmas break of my junior year, my sister Judy and her boyfriend Robert got married in Michigan. Same church, same VFW hall as Uncle Stan and Aunt Diane. Robert expected only a few family members from Georgia to attend. His little sister Sherry and I were matched as bridesmaid and groomsman.

"When she arrives," Judy suggested with an excited twinkle in her eye, "I want you to take Sherry on a date. She's only 14, and she's never been on one."

Judy was being kind in her phrasing. I knew what she meant. "You're 16 and you've never been on a date. I'm making this easy by arranging it for you."

I was excited to go on a date mostly because I had my driver's license and was curious to try to drive in snow.

The very idea of getting to take someone out for a meal and movie, without adults around, made me feel mature.

Our awkward conversation over pizza was complicated by the fact that I couldn't distinguish most of the words Sherry said in her thick Georgia accent. I found myself smiling and nodding a lot and wondering exactly what I was affirming. Sherry agreed to see the movie *Heroes*, a small picture starring Henry Winkler and Sally Field. Apparently, it was a good date movie, but I was disappointed. Based on the reviews I read, it was not likely to be nominated for any Oscars.

I ended up loving the movie. It was sweet and heartfelt, even romantic. Yet that element of it ignited no inspirations in me. During the movie, I never once entertained the idea of holding Sherry's hand or resting my arm on the back of her chair. I was busy exploring what the screenwriter was doing to get me so engrossed in a film I began watching with so little expectation of liking.

Driving home from the cinema, we passed the old S & H Green Stamps store. This was the same winding route Mom and I took the day I would have run away. Contrasting this cold night drive with the uncomfortable heat of my conversation with Mom eight years earlier made me feel so adult. I was now 16, my creative mind reeling with new ideas inspired by the movie I'd just seen, and I was handling the slick snowy road with mastery. Oh, yeah, and I had just had my first date.

As my parents had taught me, I was a conscientious gentleman. When we returned to Baka's house, where we all were staying, I opened Sherry's door for her and told her what a wonderful time I had. She politely agreed and assured me the whole evening was very "nahce."

The rest of the adults were still out, and my younger brother Ray was in the living room watching television. Baka had already gone to sleep. Sherry joined Ray in the living room while I went to Uncle Stan's old bedroom to change into my pajamas. When I returned to the living room, the television was still on, but Ray and Sherry were gone. I passed through the dark kitchen and headed toward a dim light in the breezeway at the back of the house. Even from the distance of the kitchen, I could make out two profiles, lips interlocked, over the green upholstered chair.

I slipped away unnoticed. I felt mortified. On the night of my rite of passage toward becoming a man, my little brother, who had just turned 13, was making out with the girl I just took on a date. I knew the truth: socially, I was stunted.

The next spring semester and throughout my senior year, I was determined to be more sociable. Most often, I got together with my best friend, Philip Lu. Phil was diligent, focused, and determined to be salutatorian. Like me, he was so committed to his studies, he didn't seem to indulge in much of a social life.

Though serious by nature, Phil could be funny. Phil was Korean, with a large head and lean body. Whenever anyone mistook him for being Chinese or Japanese, he would correct them and add, "It's okay, all Asians look the same." I would watch his expression after he said it. I could tell he was challenging smart people to reconsider their prejudices, and insulting ignorant people, for whom he had little patience.

On Friday nights, we would go to the local Pizza Hut for pizza and beer. At first Phil ordered mugs of beer and I would have a soft drink. Eventually, he suggested it would be more economical to buy a pitcher of beer and more fun if I drank with him. Around the time I realized that my rigid rules of conduct were mostly prompted by fear of acknowledging some truths about myself, I decided to be a little adventurous and drink with him. I never acquired a taste for beer, but I learned to appreciate first-hand the bonding effect of sharing a drink with a friend.

I loved our introspective conversations. We shared insights, rather than mere opinions about people. As an aspiring writer, I wanted to understand why people acted as they did. For me, everyone was a potential character who might show up in a work of fiction, which I had started writing more consistently my senior year. I even set a goal to write my first novel before I graduated. Left-brained and unemotional, Phil respected people he considered intelligent, and dismissed most everyone else as uninteresting. Knowing that Phil had this perspective and chose to spend most Friday nights with me did wonders for my self-esteem.

We talked often about respect. Phil gauged his opinion of everyone—classmates and teachers alike—by how much he respected them. That topic veered one conversation into the most personal of territories one night, likely encouraged by the beer. He brought up the topic of sex.

Initially, we spoke in generalities. Ours was the first generation where pregnant high school girls weren't shipped to a home for unwed mothers. Phil didn't think much of girls who allowed themselves to get pregnant in high school, but he made no such sweeping generalization about girls who had sex. "Knowing a girl has had sex isn't enough for me to question whether I could respect her."

"Have you had sex?" I asked.

Phil had an unconscious habit of threading his long, narrow fingers through his bangs before he said something personal that took courage to share. "Yes."

I was stunned.

He repeated the hand swipe through his hair and continued. "It was during a science club field trip."

"Who?"

"I told her I'd never say." I knew Phil. When he gave his word about something, he kept it.

"How was it?"

"Okay."

Okay?! I had no idea how he—or anyone—could respond so casually to the experience of having had sex. Proof of my confusion came from a recent memory. One evening not long before this conversation, Phil and I had gone bowling. In the alley next to us were two couples in their 20s. I was immediately attracted to a sandy-haired guy with a taut physique accentuated by his thin, lavender colored knit shirt. When he bowled, I couldn't stop watching him. Every movement was beautiful to me—like an athletic dance.

Near the end of the evening, with my arm extended across the chairs that backed up to the next alley, I watched Phil add our scores. Suddenly, I felt a smooth, hairy forearm brush against mine. I turned my head just enough to realize it was the beautiful lavender athlete. Unconsciously, he left his arm there. He was touching me. Another man was touching me. I remained still to savor the sensation that only I was aware of. Seconds later he moved, and the physical connection ended. But the exhilarating memory of it excited me for weeks.

As my mind drifted, reviving the ecstasy of the memory, Phil added one more insight about his having had sex. "It didn't mean anything."

His words baffled me. I had no reference point to comprehend that perspective. Although Phil was my best friend, I was too embarrassed to ask him, "How could sex not mean anything?" I had no clue what the answer could be.

25

A Blue Movie, Blueboy, and Still Blue

In the first year of their marriage, I used to visit Judy and Robert in the house they rented about ten miles from Mom and Dad's. Often, I'd stop by unannounced because I had wanted to drive my car and had few places to go. Sometimes on the way to their house I'd swing by Sound Warehouse and buy new 8-traks. One payday I bought five: Heart's *Little Queen*, Foreigner's *Double Vision*, Boston's *Don't Look Back*, Fleetwood Mac's *Rumours*, and Queen's *News of the World*. When I spread them out on her kitchen table, Judy told me that was the best way to buy music, because I would never grow tired of having bought and listened to only one.

Seeing them displayed together triggered my writer's mind. The collection seemed to reflect my personal story I was still avoiding: I had to see things differently (*Double*

Vision) and move forward (*Don't Look Back*); I had to face the social fallout (*News of the World*) and misinterpretations (*Rumours*) of who I really was once people learned I was gay. And sandwiching all the repercussions were the gay slurs of being labeled a *Little Queen*.

Judy and Robert had plenty of friends who came over to party. They always invited me to join them, but I was much younger and generally felt uncomfortable, not with them, but with myself around them. One evening I swung by and Judy was out, but Robert had some buddies over to watch a stag movie. He invited me to stay. Dad had taught us not to give in to peer pressure, so I never engaged in activities that didn't feel right to me when tempted by friends my own age. But Robert and his friends—all grown men—not only encouraged me to watch with them, but intimated that this would be a kind of rite of passage into manhood.

I had never seen porn. In my movie reference books, there were occasional nude images—Marilyn Monroe's famous pinup and even a still from the 1933 movie *Ecstasy* with Hedy Lamar's naked breasts. None of that interested me. One image that did fascinate me in the book *Talkies: A History of Cinema* was a still from *I Am Curious Yellow*. A kneeling man and woman facing each other were squeezed together in a naked embrace. Although all I could make out was the silhouette of the man's butt, it was titillating. I didn't think to pursue finding dirty magazines after seeing it, but I did watch for the movie to come on TV as a late, late night feature.

Curious, I accepted the invitation to watch the blue movie with Robert and his friends. Once Robert started the first 8-millimeter reel, I noted how poor the quality of film. The title font was too light for the background, and the up-shot angles of the first scene revealed distracting shadows in the corner of the image.

Oh, my god, I stopped myself, *Instead of paying attention to the sex, I'm re-directing the movie!* I really didn't have a clue how to enjoy the most basic of pleasures.

Finally, I started paying attention to the nude players. There were several big-busted, blonde women all insatiably attracted, simultaneously, to one guy. It might have been his uniform. Although his body was nude from the start, he was apparently a navy man because he wore a sailor hat. It remained on his head from foreplay all the way through his first climax. The movie had no sound, but the women's expressions indicated they were not just moaning with pleasure but screaming in ecstasy. I wondered why. With all these women clamoring over him like maggots on a dead bird, he lay there passively throughout most of the first reel.

Ugh! Pay attention and enjoy this! I had to remind myself again.

While Robert and his buddies commented about the women, I was watching—with fascination—the handsome sailor. He was muscular and masculine—the very kind of guy I had told myself would hate me if he knew I was attracted to him. But the second-reel action changed that thought. Another guy joined in what had become an orgy. Although both guys kept focusing on different women—or responding to the multiple women kissing their mouths and stimulating them, I was most intrigued by the times the two guys' naked bodies touched. Sometimes one guy's foot would rub against the other's leg. That seemed accidental until the other guy responded by rubbing his foot against the first guy. Sometimes, while a pile of women was working them over, they lay side by side. At one point, they pressed their round rear ends against each other. Neither jolted to move away. One of the guys even started rotating his hips. It seemed to me he was not doing it so much to position himself to penetrate a woman, but to stimulate his ass in contact with the other male's.

When the lights came up after the movie, Robert's friends marveled about the busty women. Some picked their favorite. One guy left right away, claiming he was going to ask his wife to do some of the things the most voracious actress did, quite expertly it seemed.

I didn't leave that night feeling more manly, or more bonded to Robert and his friends. I left curious and relieved. With no experience to reinforce any idea I ever had about men or intimacy, I assumed that what I felt for the kind of men I was attracted to would disgust them like my mother watching the lesbian wedding or my great aunt reading the *National Enquirer*. But these actors, who I assumed were straight because of their focus on all the females hungrily attacking them, never responded as if repulsed by the touch of another man. Instead, their reactions and further movements indicated great comfort with it. The second-reel guy even seemed excited by it. On my way home, I felt an exhilaration of hope.

But not following up with action sent me spiraling back into lonely depression. The last two songs on Heart's *Little Queen* 8-trak were "Cry to Me" and "Go on Cry." There were evenings when I'd ride alone in my first car—a used, light blue Ford LTD I nicknamed "The Blue Bomb" because it was broken down more often than it was running—and feel my heart constrict with confused heartache. I was no longer indulging in just feeling sorry for myself as I had in middle school. This sadness was deeper and more genuine. I felt vacuously lonely. But passivity is deadly. Nothing would happen until I gathered enough courage to take action and break free of my isolation by being honest, with somebody, about what I felt, and the awful things it led me to believe about myself.

At my lowest point, I was not scheduled the entire weekend at the grocery store where I worked. Instead of feeling relieved, I felt more isolated than ever. The gap between Friday afternoon when I left school and Monday morning when I'd return felt like an eternal wasteland. I couldn't stand this loneliness another day. I drove to Judy and Robert's house intent on coming out to my sister.

Determined to follow through on my intention, I immediately asked Judy if I could speak to her alone. She and I went to the living room at the front of their house, which they never used. Robert stayed away the entire time we talked.

I lay on the couch speechless. Judy's face contorted with worry. Unable to look her in the eyes and tell her, I turned to the back of the couch and started my halting confession. "I'm unclear about my feelings about guys," I tried to ease my way into the topic. Lying wasn't helping. "No," I corrected, "I'm clear about my feelings about guys. I always have been. I like them."

I paused. Judy didn't say anything. I felt even more scared now, but it was too late for a retraction. "I'm attracted to guys. I don't like girls—that way. I never have."

Still no reply from Judy. I continued. "But I've been so confused because I don't like gay guys." I was thinking of effeminate men. "I mean, I don't like feminine guys. All this time I kept thinking that meant I must not be gay, because I'm not like them, and I'm not attracted to them."

Judy finally spoke. "How long is 'all this time'?"

"Always."

I think she knew. Although we were five years apart, we always got along great. Of all her brothers, I was the only one willing to try synchronized swimming with her in our backyard pool or shop with her for her homecoming dresses.

"Have you met somebody?"

"No!" I blurted. "I've never done anything with anybody." The idea of that thought once seemed noble. Now it felt cowardly.

Finally, I blurted to another person the words that weighed me down so long. "I am so lonely."

Especially at that time, we Leslies were not physically demonstrative. But as I lay there both numb and pulsating with fear, I felt my sister gently stroke my hair. She moved my bangs aside until I felt her fingertips against the skin of my forehead. That simple human contact was the most impactful physical connection I'd ever felt.

Over the next few months, I would ask Judy back into that living room to talk more. It soon became clear that merely sharing old thoughts and feelings with her was not moving me out of the closet. I had only opened the door to show her I was in there. I needed to step out and feel the light of life that never pervaded the shadows of my secret fears.

I knew I wanted to tell my parents. Judy never encouraged or discouraged that step. Mostly she told me to try dating girls to see if maybe my feelings were wrong. "Why commit to something until you know from experience?" Her point made sense, but I knew, and always knew, exactly what I did feel for guys and didn't feel for girls. I didn't tell Judy this because since she married Robert she'd grown close to his sister, Sherry. My non-date with

Sherry confirmed through personal experience that I had no interest in girls.

Throughout my three years at Jersey Village High School, I shared my writing dreams, and some of my writing, with my English teachers. My last semester in high school, I wrote my first novel. My senior English teacher, Mrs. Collings was a blonde peanut of a woman whose pinky fingers curved inward. When she waved her hands to make a point in class, I always wondered if she would develop arthritis in her hands like Grandma Leslie.

Mrs. Collings not only read my manuscript but sacrificed several of her lunch periods to invite me to her office and discuss it. She was excited when she caught some of my symbolism, and she even read into some names biblical references that I had not intended but worked beautifully. Sharing my writing, the most important focus of my future, felt very intimate. Her supportive response made me feel safe around her. So one day I asked if I could visit her after school to tell her something.

At her house that afternoon, we sat on her front porch swing. I told her I felt conflicted about my feelings toward other guys.

"You mean homosexual feelings?"

I wondered if telling her was a mistake. Clearly, she was uncomfortable with my confession, but she was still kind. She suggested it might just be a phase I was going through. She said she would pray for me and assured me she would tell no one else what I confessed to her.

We had spent the school year talking about literature during class, and then mentioned bolder, more mature works while discussing my novel. During our lunchtime talks, she occasionally referred to other books mine reminded her of. So it didn't strike me as unusual when, after our porch swing talk, she recommended I read Thomas Mann's *Death in Venice*. Rather than simply check it out of the library, where I worked as a student assistant, I drove to the B. Dalton bookstore in The Galleria shopping mall to buy a copy. Walking down the corridor from the parking garage, I passed a magazine kiosk just past the See's Candies store. I stopped by to browse through the Hollywood magazines when another section caught my eye. They had gay magazines on display.

They were not pornographic, because they weren't shrink-wrapped. At first, I was too nervous to pick one up and look inside. But on the way back from B. Dalton, I mustered enough courage to head right to one of the gay magazines and flip through the inside. Tucking my paperback copy of *Death in Venice* under my arm helped steady my trembling hands a little. I picked up the first magazine, called *Honcho*, and was stunned to see articles and photographs of all kinds of gay men, mostly muscular and masculine. There were a few nude photos, and several of men showing only their hairy pecs. I picked up another magazine called *Blueboy*. The men featured in this magazine looked more like models. They seemed younger and blonder and more stereotypically gay. I liked the guys in the first magazine better. I didn't have the courage to buy either magazine that day, but memories of looking through them lingered enticingly in my mind until, that spring semester my senior year, I returned regularly to The Galleria just to look through the magazines. Eventually, I started buying them.

26

Something Was Still Missing

Mom had taught us all to be such good housekeepers, I never feared she would find my magazines hidden beneath my mattress. I always kept my room so clean and organized my parents never had a reason to enter it. The only other person living in our house at the time, my brother Ray, was so much more worldly and adventurous than I that he never entertained the possibility that I would have anything interesting in my room. The electric typewriter I used to write my first novel, the schoolbooks and tablets stacked on my dresser, and the classic novels arranged alphabetically by author on my bookshelf were repellent indicators that I was an uninterestingly nerdy older brother.

Although I returned to The Galleria a few times to buy new issues of both magazines that spring, I never amassed a collection. After looking through them a few times, I'd feel guilty. On trash collection day, I'd wrap them in a paper bag bound with electrical tape and drop them in our receptacle at the curb as I heard the heavy whirr and screech of the garbage truck round the street toward our house. After I dropped them in the trash, I watched from beside the garage to make sure evidence of my secret purchases were gone.

While the magazine content—especially photos of masculine men—intrigued me, they didn't sustain my attention like a good book could. After I finished reading *Death in Venice*, I felt affirmed by my teacher's recommendation. I completed the first read feeling excited to know that gay literature existed. I hadn't read any before. So hungry was I to find positive assurances about being gay, I interpreted Thomas Mann's work as a story of love so rich, the protagonist, Aschernbach was willing to die simply to be near Tadzio, the untouched object of his affection.

As we had with the book I'd written, I visited with Mrs. Collings to discuss *Death in Venice*. She never said much but kept waiting for my reaction. In my discussion, I tempered my enthusiasm and the detail of my real response. But it filled me with hope and courage. To me, Aschernbach's intense fascination with Tadzio gave his life meaning. Oblivious to the age difference of the characters, I saw Aschernbach as an example of someone who realized his passions. Rather than fight them, he nurtured them, always from a respectable proximity to Tadzio. In my mind, his death was glorious because he remained in Venice near Tadzio and was rewarded by getting to die in the presence of the young man who, for him, represented love and passion— the two qualities I felt certain would make my life meaningful when I finally felt them for a man. I left out this personal revelation from our literary discussion: The book helped me imagine admiring someone I knew, not a handsome actor in a movie or on TV, or a noble character in a book. I wanted to love a man in the flesh.

Even a cursory elaboration on my perspective of Mann's book silenced my teacher to wide-eyed panic. Though she refrained from barking her disagreement by locking her jaw and gripping the arms of her chair, I could see her eyes yelling, "No! No! No!" to my interpretation. Instead of responding, she abruptly dismissed me, and thereafter kept such a distance I knew my days of confiding in her were over.

I reread *Death in Venice* wondering what she might have meant for me to see. Exploring another perspective, I sensed that she had intended for me to realize that the wages of even unconsummated homosexual sin were, quite deservedly, death. Her bibliotherapy backfired. Instead of retreating from the advances I was making out of my oppressive closet, I felt emboldened by the book to keep finding more courage to explore my sexuality.

Before I did that, I wanted to come out to my parents. At the time, I didn't know any other gay person's story, so I didn't know how unique the stages of my coming out apparently were. Armed only with the awareness that I knew who I was and would one day search for a love who reciprocated my feelings, I had come out to my sister and a teacher. Now I needed to tell my mom and dad.

I never wanted to disappoint them. But I could not spend the rest of my life lonely and alone. Soon I *would* explore the possibilities of finding love—with another male. I knew my parents respected me. I refused to let them discover through some third party that I was out doing something that would shock and disappoint them. I felt I had to tell them what I was planning to do before I did anything.

For several days I searched so hard for the courage to come out to them I nearly made myself physically ill. When one evening my parents gave Ray permission to go with a friend to a motocross show, I felt a spiritual nudge. This was my opportunity. The closet door was ajar. I only needed enough strength to open it just far enough to let my parents know I was in there. After Ray left, I asked my parents to sit down with me because I had something important to tell them.

Mom sat in her plush Lazy-Boy rocker, and Dad sat near her at the far side of the couch. I hunkered on the floor using the coffee table as a barricade. When we first gathered, my parents seemed more curious than concerned. Surely, they knew I wasn't going to confess that I had done something immoral or illegal. I didn't spend enough time anywhere besides school and home to create that kind of trouble. As I stared at the coffee table searching for a way to start, I sensed my parents' tension rising. The gentle squeak of my mom's rocker ceased, leaving a massive silence I knew I had to fill by starting to talk.

"I have something to tell you."

They knew that. That's why we were all sitting there, with them staring at me and me studying the wood grain of the polished coffee table.

"I don't know how to start."

They didn't help with any kind of leading question or reassuring, "Whatever it is, it's okay. You can tell us anything." Rather, they just waited. I sensed there were many confessions I could make here, but some they would wish I never mentioned. Center stage, with only their worried, expectant eyes awaiting my monologue, I suddenly realized I wasn't doing this for them. I was doing it for me. No matter what their reaction, I would have to live with it and move on. But I only wanted to do that with my parents' knowledge.

Eventually I couldn't even hear them breathing. I had to begin by saying *something*. "I've had feelings I've been struggling with my entire life."

I hoped just starting to speak would open a valve inviting an entire scene to flow. When writing my novel, that often happened and resulted in some of my most dynamic and eloquent passages. That didn't happen when talking to my parents.

"I've been very clear all along about what I like. But when I was young, I didn't know what it meant. I know now."

Without a clearer context, I felt I was spinning my parents in a confused circle. Dad might not have caught where I was heading, but my mom probably knew all along. "You think you're gay?"

I looked up. She was staring at me, knowingly clear-eyed. My dad sat silent and gulped as if easing a wave of nausea.

"Yes," I said.

Finally, Dad jumped in. "How could you know? You've never even dated a girl."

"I know," I said, more firmly. I wasn't talking to my dad. I was looking right into my mother's eyes, because I knew, from her comment and my lifetime of having clung to and hung around her, that she knew, too. Her question sealed that confirmation.

"It's not that I don't like girls. I've always gotten along great with them. I just don't like them in a romantic way." I was hoping my mother might ask, "But that's how you feel about boys?" so I wouldn't have to say it. She didn't. Instead, she curled her lips sideways. I saw no wonder or concern in her expression, but a conclusive disdain. What she always knew, she still didn't want to be true.

"I don't want to spend the rest of my life without love. I want to find someone I can love and someone who'll love me. That someone can only be another male."

"How do you know that's what you want if you haven't even dated girls?"

My dad is a very intelligent man. In business, he could think on his feet, develop a compelling argument, and deliver it with such conviction that he almost always got others to agree with his perspective, or at least agree to get out of his way while he followed through with exactly what he planned to do. The repetition of his question made me think he was not only blindsided by my comment but bulldozed by it. My parents' different responses confirmed only one fact: no matter how long she suspected, she never mentioned it to my father.

"I haven't done anything," I assured them. "I never met anybody. I don't have any friends who are . . ." I realized in my hesitation that I was coming out to my parents without ever speaking the word "gay"—only my mother had said it. ". . . gay." I said it. I said the word. "But I've prayed about this a long, long time. I'm clear about what I feel, and I'm certain that I want to explore these feelings."

"If you've prayed about it, then you know it's wrong." Like Clarence Darrow, my father seemed to have latched onto a line of argumentation with traction. But I'd seen *Inherit the Wind*. Darrow was the defense attorney with the logical approach to religion.

"No, Dad. Not for me."

"You can't know. You have no experience." He rubbed the corner of his mouth in frustration. I think he realized he just encouraged me to do exactly what I just said I was going to.

I capitalized on my advantage. "Exactly. That's why I'm going to explore this. I know what I've always known about myself. But I've been afraid to face it, and then to admit it, and then to experience it. I was depressed a long time. This is what I was depressed about."

"Then why pursue it? If it makes you depressed, it couldn't be right for you."

"*Not* facing it depressed me. For a while I didn't even want to live. But I do want to live. And I want to live with love in my life."

"You already have a family."

"I'm lonely." Saying the words aloud dissipated their power. "I don't want to be lonely anymore."

"Did someone influence you? Did something happen?"

"No, Dad. I've never done anything with anyone. Now I want to. But before I do, I wanted you both to know how I feel and what I'm planning. I would never want you to find out the wrong way. It used to be a secret. It's not anymore."

That was the wrong thing to say. My parents' eyes shot spotlights of panic in my direction.

"Now you know."

"Who else knows?" Mom asked.

"I told Judy," I confessed. There seemed no point in telling them about my discussions with Mrs. Collings. Clearly those were over.

"What if I paid for you to see a psychiatrist? Do you think that would help?" My dad was still working on new arguments.

"I don't. I'm happier now, and even curious to see what life will bring."

The optimism of my inflection struck us all. It filled me with hope. But my parents looked dismayed. I think they couldn't believe I seemed so at peace with information worthy of their disappointment, and the world's disgust.

My mother pulled out the one argument she probably thought could force me to reconsider. "Boża will punish you for it."

My indifference to her comment made me realize how far I'd come spiritually reconciling who I was. She was talking to me as if I were still a little boy. I disagreed with what she said, but I didn't want to argue with her. I felt relieved that my parents took the news as well as they did. I wasn't about to pick a fight.

As withered and frightened as I felt starting the conversation, I walked upstairs to my room feeling like a man. I told my parents the truth about who I was, and I shared the insight *before* I acted on it. I was gay not because of what I did. I hadn't done anything. I knew I was gay because I had struggled with my awareness until I found the strength to acknowledge who I was. Although I thought better of myself for facing my fears and coming out to four people, including my parents, I didn't feel lighter or happier. Something was still missing, and I didn't know what.

27

On the Verge of an Emotion

I had a sweet friend named Beverly Jones who worked at Laurel's Ice Cream Shop next to the Eagle grocery store. On breaks from work, I'd head over to see her and buy me a scoop or two. I was shy and serious, but Bev and her coworkers tended to be outrageous. As they were closing the ice cream shop one night, Bev and a male coworker decided to see if she could stuff him into the horizontal display cooler atop the closed ice cream cartons with all the angled doors closed.

They forgot to lock the entrance door at closing time, so I walked in to see Bev laughing hysterically and, encased in his ice cream tomb, a long, skinny guy stretched from one end of the cooler to the other fogging up the glass as his cold face turned pink.

I often wished I could find such behavior funny like so many of my peers at the time, but I just didn't. Bev knew it. In front of her coworkers, she liked to cut up and didn't care what I thought. But one-on-one, we had some sincere, heartfelt conversations. One time, she was mopping Laurel's when I jumped over the puddle she'd created, caught the edge of the waterline and skidded a little. I broke my fall but felt embarrassed by my clumsy attempt. She read my embarrassment as something else and said in a reassuring tone, "Don't worry. I think you're masculine. And most people don't care."

I wasn't sure I heard her right. *Don't care? About what?* We stared at each other for an awkward moment, as if she were waiting for me to catch onto to the message she was trying to convey with diplomacy. I got it, but then felt even more self-conscious that my clumsiness must have looked feminine to her. Bev and I never said anything more about my masculinity, but she became the first person who told me, if only through a veiled assurance, that she knew I was gay. When my prom night neared, I asked Bev to be my date.

"Sure I'll go . . ." then she added ". . . friend" to clarify the parameters of this *date*.

The prom was downtown at the Hyatt Regency, one of the first open-air lobbies where every floor had a visible ledge lined with tiny lights that matched those that rose up and down the glass elevators. Stepping into the ballroom with Bev got me approving looks and gestures from male classmates. Bev was a year younger than I, and she attended a rival school in the district. She was also very pretty.

Bringing Bev implied to my classmates that I had more of a personal life than they knew. They never saw me at Tin Hall or other teen hangouts because I was never invited, and because I had no desire to go clubbing. I never talked about Bev at school because she wasn't my girlfriend, just a dear friend I saw when I worked, or occasionally when we went out to play pinball at a local arcade.

For the length of the event, I let my male classmates think I was straight because I liked the rare pleasure of feeling affirmed by them. The aftertaste of their approval was bitter. I knew they were responding to my lie of omission.

But their approval was not the one that stung most. Early that evening, I picked up Bev and brought her back to our house because my mother wanted photos of Bev and me all dressed up and heading out together. As Mom posed us for pictures on the stairs, I realized my parents were almost giddy for me. They never gushed like this when Judy, their eldest child and only daughter, went to her milestone dances. I knew why they were excited, and I felt guilty. They thought this "date" with Bev negated my coming out. After that conversation only a few weeks earlier, we never talked more about my being gay. Now, going to the prom with a girl seemed to erase for them everything I had said about how I struggled and who I was. To their apparent relief, they seemed to think everything had changed.

I returned home late the night of my prom to find my parents still awake. They wanted to hear the details of my date. They looked at me with such loving expectation, I felt like a failure and liar. It was one thing to let male classmates whom I barely knew think something false about me. It felt totally disingenuous to lie to my mom and dad. I was heartsick. I didn't meet their level of enthusiasm in my reply. I simply told them my friend Bev and I had a very nice time, and I was glad I went.

That night in bed, I tried starting a dialog with God, but I was too emotional. Trouble was, the emotion didn't reveal anything to me because I didn't know what I was feeling. Guilty? Sad? Disappointed? Frustrated? I tossed in bed awhile, then finally wrapped myself tight in my blanket and came to the clearest conclusion I could draw: I felt on the verge of an emotion I couldn't identity.

28

Light

The next night I didn't sleep at all. My body shook
with agitation. I couldn't resume my dialog with God
because my ears were ringing and my head hurt. The air in
my bedroom felt stifling. That emotion I couldn't identify
was stuck in my throat until I couldn't swallow. I had had it.
I was so ready for a breakthrough I got out of bed well before
dawn and raced to the church early, early Sunday morning.
There, I was determined to come to terms with whatever God
and I still had to resolve.

Even though the sky was still dark, the front doors of
St. Matthew's were open. Inside, recessed lights soft as a
whisper lit pinpoints of the sanctuary. I suspected somebody
had to be there, but I saw no one. In the cry room not one
votive was lit. That's where I wanted to be. It was so dark in

that interior space I had to feel my way toward a plush pew. I fumbled to my usual pew and knelt.

I never thought of prayer as confrontation, but instead of folding my hands, I curled my fists as if ready to fight. I was angry. That was the emotion I couldn't identify that had kept me riled all weekend! I felt anger—at God, the world, religion, my family, myself. But in my mind, anger expressed the antithesis of love, and ultimately, I craved love. As emotion welled, I short-circuited it with another question. How could I ever hope to find love through simmering, unexpressed anger?

My thoughts reeled. I was exhausted by the futile attempts to inch my way out of the closet that went nowhere. My sister and I didn't feel any closer. I panicked my English teacher by misinterpreting *Death in Venice*. I gave my parents false hope by taking a girl to the prom.

In that moment I made a decision, consequences (and my soul?) be damned. I gave up my staunch adherence to the tenets of what I learned from my parents and grandmothers and the nuns who taught us at St. Linus. I didn't care if I lusted. I didn't care if I hated. I didn't care of Boża punished me. I didn't care if what I thought and felt struck me dead with a bolt of lightning. Even at age 18, theoretically with so much of life ahead of me, I would rather have suffered a quick death than linger without hope and with the tornadic emotions that clouded and confused me.

In that desolate cry room, my thoughts dissolved under a sudden eruption of fury. I could feel my emotions filling the cry room, tight and threatening like an overblown balloon.

I did not punch a hole through a window or take a box-cutter from work and slash angry symbols into the backs of the upholstered pews. I yanked off my sweater, pressed it into my face, and yelled. I had no idea if a priest or altar boys would enter the church during my long tirade. If anyone found me in this posture of upheaval, I didn't care. I hollered into the thick pile of my sweater. No words or expletives sifted through the muffling weave. No tears streamed from my eyes. Instead, power surged through me. My body shook. My nerve endings jolted through fingers clutching that wadded sweater. I have never been able to carry a tune, but I could feel a gale force baritone fury hurricaning from my lungs.

I don't know how long my self-imposed scream therapy lasted. When I finally took the sweater from my face, I was still alone in the church. But to my surprise, the room where I hid and prayed was no longer dark and pressure packed. Instead, in a sweep of joy that felt miraculous, light filled the closet with bright calm. In fact, the entire church was gently illuminated like a field outside Lourdes.

The light was not rising up and rotating like the Hollywood spotlight I had told Baka was God. As Sister James Marie taught, it didn't seem to be coming from the sky. It simply permeated the room so quietly and fully I felt as if the light were filling me to the point where I might well be invisible.

My mind knew there was likely a physical explanation. When my face was buried in my sweater, the sun had probably risen. The double doors along either side of the building might be open and letting in morning sunbeams. Now within an hour of the first mass, someone may have turned on the interior lights. More likely, they were set to come on automatically.

But the science of what was happening made it no less a miracle. I raised my head, opened my eyes, and the dark had been replaced with light. I didn't see visions of God, but I felt spiritually full. In that moment, I quit judging myself for being gay and let God love me as one made in the image and after the likeness of God. If God could love me, I could, too.

As the Bible suggested, I did go into the closet to pray. My isolation—my time in the desert—led me to discard what I had been taught so I could find God myself. So many catechisms I thought didn't apply to me as a gay boy finally illuminated my own path. I not only belonged to the human race, but I could contribute to it only by being and living exactly as God made me. In the cocoon of that cry room, my muffled scream broke open the chrysalis and showed me the light.

The pattern of brightness suggested that the source of all the light was emanating from the cry room. To my marveling eyes, it spread like inexplicably multiplying loaves and fishes throughout the sanctuary. Awestruck I asked God, *Did this light come out of the closet to illuminate the whole church?*

That morning, my dialogs with God stopped being one-sided. Deep within I sensed more than heard God answer, "No, the light came out of Me, through you."

Then God instructed me what to do with that epiphany. "In private, build your faith in Me. In public, have the courage to be who I made you. Let My light shine."

AFTERWORD

Years later I had a soul-expanding conversation with a beloved aunt who has always been my model of faith. Despite divergent interpretations of spirituality, we always reach the same conclusion: God is thriving, dynamic love. Standing alone in my parents' kitchen, I told her I was gay. By this time, I was in my 20s and had been with my husband Jerry several years, so the revelation was not surprising to her. But opening to her with that fact brought us an even greater bond than we already shared.

Her immediate response intrigued me. "Don't tell your uncle." Like most successful and happy couples, she and her husband had learned to create a cohesive union from opposite personalities. Their differences included disagreeing about who or what God is and how or if God impacts our lives.

She then offered her version of words of understanding and compassion. "Like all of us, we come to this life with a cross to bear. Being gay is yours."

No! I thought. *This is not a cross at all. It's been the greatest gift because it led to—even demanded that I examine my own thoughts and emotions so deeply I finally discovered my soul.*

As she elaborated on her comment, I realized, through her devout Catholic perspective, she was sharing her own interpretation of the same positive message. In the years since I dissociated from Catholicism in search of a spiritual path that affirmed and encouraged my spiritual journey, thanks to my sweater-muffled epiphanies, I recognized negative connotations I'd adopted to the Catholic symbols for suffering and atonement. But from my aunt, who not only adhered to but thrived spiritually thanks to those symbols, I appreciated her perspective, and even rediscovered how integrally every step of my journey since birth contributed to where I am now, and where I am yet to reach.

Her cross is, in my vernacular, my challenge. It's the scenario of conflict that I interpret as a force with which to struggle until I grow and regain my peace and equilibrium at each subsequent expanded, heightened, and deepened spiritual plateau.

I wonder, are they actually plateaus? The analogy works for me, as it seems that after each new revelation, I find solid footing again after a period of emotional tumult.

The more I live, the less tornadic the storm of emergence toward my next spiritual epiphany. Last night I had a dream that quite neatly encapsulates this pattern of temporary disarray to a new, more powerful awareness of my place in the Paradise that is life when I look through Godlike eyes.

I was in the middle of moving from my childhood home, the interior of which was a dense mountain range of half-packed belongings. That day, the people who had bought the house started receiving mail at that address. I went to the front porch to find mounds of mail that matched the mountain range inside. In the middle of the cement porch I saw a leather belt. It was only half-complete, like a middle school shop project a student didn't plan well enough to finish. Like the belt itself, the engraving was not quite finished either. The first words were burnt into the leather, uniform and easy to read. They trailed off in quality and legibility and concluded with the last letters added in pencil.

But the message left me breathless. It read:

I am God. I did it all. The next move is mine, too.

I look at my life from the perspective of that message and realize that everything, everything is a gift. Most dynamically, my spiritual awareness is the greatest of those gifts because it enables me to appreciate the message etched into that leather. The power that ignited the universe to set everything in perfect, synchronized motion is greater than anything anyone can think or feel or do. It is as immutable as scientific law. Its power contains the opportunities we all have that some call our crosses to bear and others call their challenges, and ultimately are the routes we find to discover our own soul.

We may notice God, even passively revere God, in the gentle slope of a flower petal, but we ignite our desire for, even need of God, while caged in brambles.

As an adult, I have been a relentless optimistic. I strive to surge with enthusiasm for life every moment of my day. Early in the morning, my husband Jerry asks me to turn down the volume of my enthusiasm. Colleagues refer to me as "so dang upbeat." I am most proud when people tell me I'm the happiest person they know. Jerry agrees, and has concluded that it comes from my living in Rogerland. It is a place I'm proud to claim because I created it.

How? Was I born this happy? No, but like all of us, I was born with the potential to be and think and feel anything I choose. What led me to make this choice and commit to it so steadfastly? I owe it all to the long, dark night of my soul that consumed my teen years.

As an optimist, I spent much of my adulthood rejecting the concept of a dark night altogether. I resented philosophers who suggested that we had to go through some awful trauma or suffer severe setbacks to feel the first glimmer of enlightenment. But in my previous book, *Divine Destiny*, I spent much time exploring the Genesis story of The Garden of Eden. In it, Adam and Eve eat of the Tree of The Knowledge of Good and Evil, recognize their nakedness, and banish themselves from Paradise.

Nearly all religious and spiritual traditions have a similar legend about humans having and then losing Paradise. To punish humanity, a divine character or committee hides Heaven. In the Catholic legend, that character is a king. According to the Native American Sioux, it's an eagle. Hindus call it Brahma. Most traditions refer to that character as God.

The legend traces God (or God's committee) deciding where to hide Heaven. God considers hiding

Heaven on the top of a mountain, at the bottom of the sea, or deep inside the earth. God rules out those options as too easy to find. But as the legend concludes, and Jesus confirmed, the Kingdom of Heaven is within. God put Heaven inside us all. We are carrying Heaven around with us. The challenge and glory of this life is rediscovering Heaven.

Why would that be necessary? If we're born into Heaven, why not just bask in it always? Because we can never appreciate the full value of Heaven without having co-created it with God. As reflections of God, we are creative energy. We cannot fully appreciate what is merely handed to us. To truly value anything, we must contribute to its creation. We want to earn our place among the seraphim.

We come to this life aware of Heaven, but not fully attuned to the fact we're already in it. Armed with our free will, we traverse through the dark night of our soul so we can then awaken to the Paradise this universe always was, is, and ever shall be.

A combination of circumstances paves the way into and then through our dark night. Being gay would seem the catalyst for my dark night. It wasn't. It was my fear of never having love. The convergence of a subtle awareness of feeling somehow unique in how I related to both sexes led my young mind to latch onto every snarl, jibe, and disparaging comment about homosexuality. Even so young, I was marking my path out of Paradise.

From a worldly perspective, I might have concluded that a series of poor choices robbed me of Paradise. Unidentified rebellion made my school grades plummet. Youthful immaturity confused my fear of Sister James Marie with the false conclusion that she didn't like me. Yet all these years later I remember how she chastised me and others. Why? Because she invited me to find my own courage, and I shrunk from it. Our angels are not always gentle allies.

When Aunt Diane took me to the altar to cry out for Jesus, I concluded that He didn't hear me. But God was there, in the form of a tan, curly blond-haired man I feared would judge me, when I wanted, oh, how I wanted, someone like him to love me.

One-by-one, I discarded all grade-school friendships. Until I wrote this memoir, I have remembered myself in those last years at St. Linus as lonely and isolated. To verify some names for this book, I found my 8th grade memory book, a home-spun version of a yearbook. I was shocked to see that in it, I was selected from among my peers as Most Talented and Most Artistic. Even more surprising, I was singled out for my ability to make friends. The dark night of the soul is filled with misperceptions about ourselves. But I have come to appreciate that making what seemed at the time to be human errors is our soul's way of creating the return path through our dark night right back into Paradise.

I have always considered the nadir of my life my freshman year at Divine Child. On reflection, I see a sad and lost 14-year-old. But writing about that year now, I see everything from a brighter perspective. Even though I didn't recognize it, I always had solid support. At the time, my greatest need was to earn the admiration of my teachers. My fifth-period gym coach, who saw me at my worst, was also my first-period English teacher. Every day he saw me excel in the subject of my lifelong passion *before* I stumbled through my athletic shortcomings. Yet in that gym class I met my Samson.

Also, in two different classes I was taught by the loving Miss Croskey. On my last day, she gave me a copy of *Jonathan Livingston Seagull*. My earliest imaginings of being a writer were shaped by novels like *The Great Gatsby* and *The Heart is a Lonely Hunter*. I didn't know, but Spirit did, that my greatest contributions as a writer would come through inspirational works. Go to any bookstore, and you'll find many more of my books next to Richard Bach than you will beside F. Scott Fitzgerald or Carson McCullers. My introduction to that genre came as a gift from my religion teacher.

I never had male instructors until Divine Child. I started and ended my day in classes taught by two men I found handsome. My last period algebra teacher, Mr. Carroll, championed my perfect GPA the day I checked out of Divine Child. In childhood, I hungered for men to notice and acknowledge me. Mr. Carroll did.

On my last day in his class, I also met Fran Cyburt, a lifelong friend and fellow bibliophile. Of course. Looking back from my spot in Paradise, it was meant to be.

Throughout my life, I have contended that moving across the country saved my life. While sinking in the mire of self-pity, I had an opportunity to start anew. My naiveté helped save my life. Had I known that I wouldn't really start digging myself out of the dark night of my soul until I hit rock-bottom while alone at St. Matthew's church one early Sunday morning nearly three years later, I might have acted on my suicidal thoughts.

But everything, everything happening on the physical plane is prompted by Spirit to guide us toward claiming our place in Paradise. The Universe provides us with Heaven at birth. But as reflections of God, we must claim Heaven ourselves.

As humans we learn best through contrast. So, we are emboldened to full appreciation of what we have by the awareness or experience of loss. Knowing we will physically die invites awareness of what is here and now. Facing our own dark night gives us the experience of loss that ultimately leads us to fulfill the purpose of our free will: to choose and reclaim the Paradise that we really never lost, but simply didn't have the resources to appreciate.

Once we have survived one genuine dark night, we emerge from it enlightened. With that first glimpse of enlightenment, nothing can scare us spiritually anymore. There will be more worldly challenges, but in Paradise we know why they come and what purpose they serve. From that perspective, we see them as welcome blessings.

We are never given a challenge we are not already equipped and ready to conquer. In those challenges are blessings that our Soul recognizes as angels, even if our worldly perspective doesn't. I am blessed because through my dark night I had angels like Sister James Marie and Aunt Diane and Samson and Miss Croskey and Mr. Carroll and

Fran guiding me. Though I didn't know it at the time, every prayer was being answered before I asked it. Paradise was always present waiting patiently for me to realize I never left.

AFTERWARD

It's been more than four decades since I emerged from my dark night and fell in love with life by reconciling who I am. So many people shaped that journey. Here's what's become of them.

FAMILY

Both Judy and Ray live not far from me, and Randy is still in Michigan. In 2016, Mom died of congestive heart failure with Dad, Judy, and a hospice nurse at her bedside. Last December 1, I moved Dad, aged 90, to a senior independent living facility. The next Saturday, I shared the best day I ever had with my brothers as we cleared out the family home we moved to in 1976. We found, and reminisced about, mementoes of our childhood my parents saved from our earliest days in Michigan. Today, as I proofread this manuscript the last time, Dad and Ray are signing the papers to complete the sale of that house.

GRANDMOTHERS

Six years after my family moved to Texas, Baka died in her sleep. A cousin had been coming over to paint the trim on her house. One morning he couldn't get a response from his knocking on the locked door. He crawled in her bedroom window and found her dead. She died in the bed from which, at the start of those few years in the mid-1970s, Baka would call to me, "Happy New Year, honey."

In January of 1990, Grandma Leslie died at home after battling colorectal cancer. My dad, aunt, and two of Grandma's sisters were there to hear her last breath.

AUNTS AND UNCLES

Aunt Diane divorced Uncle Stan just months after she was born again. From Christmas cards she wrote Mom over the years, we learned Diane married a preacher. They moved to North Dakota and had four sons. I don't know if Mrs. Martinez lived long enough to make the move with them.

Uncle Stan retired early from his pipefitter job at Ford Motor Company and moved to Cadillac, Michigan with his motorcycle, wave runner, snow mobile, and a black German shepherd mix named Tutai, a Polish word that translated to spy. I never learned where he came up with the name, or what it meant to him. When Uncle Stan was only 57, he died on his sofa from a heart attack. He lay there two days before his neighbor found him.

Aunt Bev died even younger. The drugs started eating away at her organs in 1988. At age 42, she went into a coma and died a week later.

My confirmation sponsor Uncle Tom succumbed to COPD just months before my mom died. Aunt Arlene, his wife and my godmother, still lives in Michigan.

FRIENDS

Cathy Farchione, the neighbor girl with whom I used to play house and Barbies, is a Facebook friend. Just yesterday she responded to one of my posts. Her mother still lives on the cul-de-sac where we grew up. On trips to Michigan, I drive around Dearborn Heights to reminisce. If I see Mrs. Farchione's car in their driveway, I stop in to visit and give her a copy of my latest book.

I didn't try to rebuild any friendships with former classmates from St. Linus. Most, like Linus Erlingus, Mary Pat "Michael" Brogan, and Patti Kwatera, are tucked comfortably in my past. Thanks to social media, I've recently reconnected with some St. Linus alum, including Steve Hideg and John Machniak.

I have only one permanent bond from Divine Child. Fran Cyburt Beckman lives in Colorado. Over the years our unbroken communication evolved from letters to emails to phone calls. She and I remain best of friends. Because I didn't even remember their names, I have no way of finding my Samson from gym class or the *Playgirl* poser with whom I shared that mysterious lingering glance during the "We hate Ohio State" pep rally chant. But I remember them both fondly.

Heading to different colleges, Philip Lu and I lost track of each other. About twenty years later, I saw his picture in the Health section of the newspaper. He had become a revered surgeon.

Bev Jones lives across the state from me. Every few years we call each other. Recently she came to town. She took me to see her mom, who lives within a few miles of my current house. We passed the afternoon looking at prom pictures.

TEACHERS

When I started undergraduate classes as an education major, I telephoned my sophomore English teacher Adele McClendon from Jersey Village High School to thank her for her inspiration. We planned to meet for dinner after her busy semester ended. She was killed in an automobile accident weeks after our conversation. I stayed in contact with my senior English teacher, Mrs. Collings throughout my undergraduate years. Soon after, we lost touch.

In 2002, while two of Randy's sons were attending Divine Child, I was invited to give a motivational speech at their assembly. Mr. Foye, the art teacher who played Elton John music during class, was still on the faculty. He was my only former teacher I saw that day. I don't know what happened to Coach Bognar or Sister Cynthia or Mr. Carroll. Over the years I've unsuccessfully searched online for Miss Croskey to thank her for her kindness to me back then. Every time I've moved, I pare down my home library collection. I still have and cherish the copy of *Jonathan Livingston Seagull* she gave me. Recently Sister Cecilia, the one who vacillated between giving me an A or A- on my final freshman report card, retired as principal of Divine Child Elementary School.

A few years after moving to Texas, I took a trip to Michigan and stopped by St. Linus School. I visited with Sister Clement Marie, who had become principal. I never did know what happened to Sister Ellen Maria. Through a serendipitous set of circumstances, I recently discovered that a Unity minister in Florida had attended Divine Child and St. Linus. I messaged him. After several failed attempts, we finally conversed by phone. The very day we talked he learned that Sister Lidwina, our elementary math teacher, had died. She was 103.

ME

I officially came out and began interacting among other gay people only two months after I saw the light emanating from that cry room. At the back of a copy of *Blueboy*, I found a personal ad from a 26-year-old seeking friends in the Houston area. I wrote a response, but then agonized several days before sending it. Once I dropped my letter in the mailbox, I felt both terrified and bold. There was no turning back. Coming to terms with God about my sexuality took one level of courage. Telling my parents I was gay took another. But sending that letter was declaring to the world who I was. The safety net of secrecy was gone.

Quite promptly, I received a kind reply from a guy named Fernando. We arranged to meet. Immediately recognizing my inexperience, he never took advantage of my naiveté. Instead, he showed me around a popular gay dance club called The Copa where he encouraged me to return to meet other gay people.

Intent on becoming an author, I started undergraduate school as an English major. Mid-degree, advice from an acquaintance led me to switch majors to English education. The change proved serendipitous in two ways.

First, in one education class I met a gracious and attractive divorced dad named Jerry. He'd recently left his job as a Methodist minister to become a teacher so he could have his two young children not just every other weekend, but all summer. Once we became friends, I learned he left the ministry because he knew he was gay. A year later, we fell in love. Jerry and I, our children Cory and Rebecca, and now our daughters-in-law and five grandchildren, have been a thriving family ever since. Jerry and I considered ourselves married since 1984. We wed in Canada in 2007.

Second, more than a decade as a teacher shaped me and my life's mission. My gloriously loving students taught me about diversity and compassion, themes that informed my writing and accelerated my search for a spiritual home.

With my Catholic background and Jerry's Methodist roots, we tried each other's churches as a couple. Neither gave us the spiritual light to explore as we wanted. After visiting many diverse churches, we found a supportive environment in Unity. After years as educators, Jerry spent 15 years as senior minister at a Unity church, and I finally realized my lifelong dream of being a full-time author. While I have had success with books in a multitude of genres, the one that draws the most from me, and resonates most with readers, is spirituality.

Index of Personal Connections to Roger Leslie

General Index

About the Author

Dr. Roger Leslie is an author, editor, publisher, and inspirational teacher. He discovered his life's mission following the light that emerged from his youthful struggle to reconcile his sexual orientation with his spirituality. Once he found his soul, he has lived from it to inspire people to live the life they dream and empower them to follow their unique spiritual destiny.

To subscribe to Leslie's email or learn more about his books and inspirational courses, visit **RogerLeslie.com**.

Courses by Roger Leslie

FLY

Based upon the principles he learned living his First Last Year, Roger Leslie developed **FLY** Courses.

Imagine living a full year as if it were your last. Done from choice instead of a fatal prognosis, you are free to *really live*. That's what it means to **FLY**.

In FLYght, you

- Clarify your purpose
- Fulfill your passions
- Embrace the present moment
- Stay spiritually awake
- Discover your Paradise
- Achieve profound personal success
- Live your destiny.

Course #1: FLY Wright

FLY Wright immerses you in living your First Last Year (FLY) now. Personalized activities clarify and prioritize what you love and value so you can immediately pursue what you've always wanted.

Course #2: FLY Air-Heart

FLY Air-Heart enhances each moment of living and immerses you in the life you dream through heart-centered explorations of what makes you happiest and most fulfilled.

Course #3: FLY Arm-Strong

FLY Arm-Strong is the empowerment phase of FLYing. Clear on the success path you've chosen, you will accelerate you progress and expand your vision to bolder, more exciting possibilities for your grandest goals.

Course #4: Shepherd Your FLYght

Once you're soaring toward your own goals and dreams, you can Shepherd Your FLYght by tapping into the interconnectedness and mutual support of all life. In this workshop, you will expand and apply your personal mission that will leave a legacy to the world.

To subscriber to Leslie's email or sign up for **FLY** courses, visit **RogerLeslie.com**.

Courses by Roger Leslie

From Inspiration to Publication

Leslie packs decades of experience as an author, editor, and publisher into this dynamic virtual workshop that empowers you to reach your next writing, publishing, or book marketing goals.

Whether your book is complete, in process, or a still-unrealized dream, this workshop provides the insights and strategies to give you meaningful progress anywhere along your writing and publishing journey.

With Leslie's guidance and the support of other authors, you will

- Clarify where you are in the writing/publishing process
- Confirm what else is required to reach success
- Identify precise goals that will provide new momentum for achievement
- Determine your timeline for success
- Solidify a plan of action to reach your goals on time

- Take the first steps to ensure you're progressing toward your clarified vision.

In addition to providing tools and templates to keep you progressing toward completion and publication, this workshop invites networking and support opportunities so all attendees can build on each other's success.

To subscriber to Leslie's email or sign up for his writing workshops, visit **RogerLeslie.com**.

CPSIA information can be obtained
at www.ICGtesting.com
Printed in the USA
LVHW032013260523
748165LV00010B/165